COURAGE
AND LOVE FOR CHILDREN
IN SOUTH AFRICA

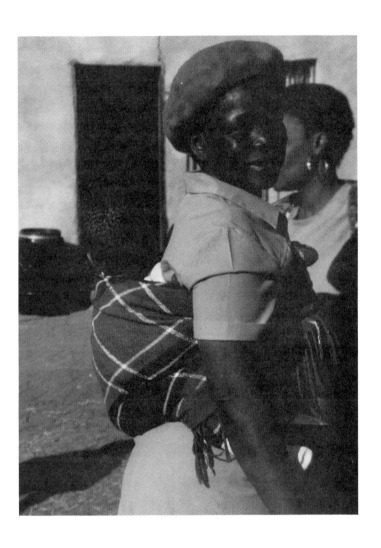

TRUUS GERAETS

COURAGE
AND LOVE FOR CHILDREN
IN SOUTH AFRICA

SCHAUMBURG PUBLICATIONS, INC.
ROSELLE, ILLINOIS 60193

With special thanks to my friend Barbara Benz for all her involvement with this book.

Photo credits: p. 59—Regula Aegler; pp. 25, 52, 122, 142b—Dr. Christhilde Blume; p. 150a—Hanno Gauger; pp. 10, 75, 94, 111, 113, 114—Truus Geraets; pp. 81, 134b, 141—Lea Holtz; pp. 90, 108—Carol Liknaitzki; pp. ii, 139, 142a—Ursula Schumann; pp. x, 150b—Cindy Spencer; pp. 61, 63a/b, 88, 99—Martin Wigand; pp. 42, 44, 69b, 100a/b, 130b, 134a—Claartje Wijnbergh; f/b cover, pp. 5, 34a/b, 73b—Michiel Wijnbergh.

Quotations from the poem "In the Amphitheater of Africa" reprinted by permission of Chris Foster and the publisher, Integrity International.

Library of Congress Cataloging-in-Publication Data

Geraets, Truus.
Library of Congress Cataloging-in-Publication Data

Geraets, Truus.
    Courage and love for children in South Africa / Truus Geraets.
        p.   cm.
    Includes bibliographical references (p.   ).
    ISBN 0-935690-04-2
    1. Blacks--Education (Elementary)--South Africa. 2. Kindergarten--South Africa. 3. Waldorf method of education--South Africa.
    I. Title.
    LC2808.S7G47   1993
        372.968--dc20   93-30475
                                                            CIP

ISBN 0-935690-04-2

CONTENTS

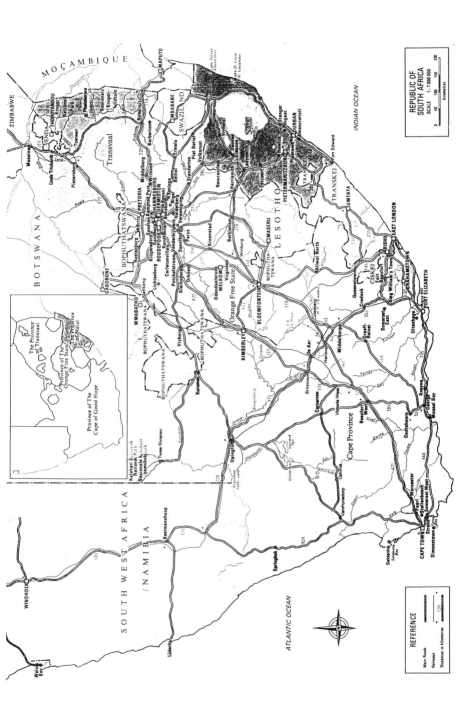

REPUBLIC OF
SOUTH AFRICA
SCALE   1:7 000 000

REFERENCE

Main Roads
Railways
Distances in kilometres

FOREWORD

In 1988 Truus Geraets published a small booklet *Stars and Rainbows over Alexandra*[1] in which she chronicled her and her colleagues' work in South Africa. Now, five years later, she reports on the sprouting and development of those early seeds.

In order to more fully present the dedicated work done by so many people under very difficult circumstances and to better show the amount of courage they had to muster to accomplish what they did and continue to do, we are including information provided by Truus Geraets in her previous writing.

At the outset of her work in South Africa she wrote:

> We people of this earth are foreigners to each other. We will remain foreigners to each other until we have learned to fully accept one another in all the facets of this foreignness. . . .
>
> When we start to reach out to people of other cultures and races, the foreignness of essential living concepts may, at times, be so overwhelming that there seems to be no connecting point. It is at this point that these differences which could just be a threshold, become a solid wall. . . .
>
> I am a real foreigner in South Africa, an alien. That is why I can see the threshold, but have not yet had the time nor the wish to build a solid brick wall around my heart.
>
> Our adventure in working together with black people in South Africa has helped me cross the threshold of our limited social concepts to meet the full-fledged human beings on the other side.
>
> To be able to keep the joy of living, to be able to still sing the song of life under the most dreadful circumstances, to still have the zest to live after centuries of being dominated, that is the strength of the black people. It is their strength and dignity that carries them through and . . . could lead them and us to a land of promise.

Truus Geraets concluded her introduction to *Stars and Rainbows over Alexandra*:

> Our work is based on the goodwill of so many people who

from far and near all are part of the project. . . . who all are trying to create oases of goodwill. Within the existing structures, the new is beginning to manifest itself in a modest way, yet as a new reality.

The kinds of seeds Truus Geraets and her friends were able to plant and nurse into growth are described in the present book.

E. Lauterbach

INTRODUCTION

In the amphitheater of (South) Africa, two peoples,
Mutually fearful, mutually dependent,
Struggle with bonds of resentment and greed
While the whole world watches,
Waits,
Condemns,
Mostly condemns.
They could be bound with bonds of love,
See the worth in each other,
See not inferiority, nor superiority
But parts of one beautiful design.
It is late, but not too late
For a New Age in Africa.

Chris Foster
"In the Amphitheater of Africa"

After living and working in South Africa for almost nine years, I became more and more convinced that Africa has a tremendous gift to give to the world. It is a gift that is unique; more so, it is essential for the rest of the world. It is the gift of strong social consciousness. The world cannot do without it. Therefore I say: Africa we need you!

My experiences are based on close working relationships and friendships with black and colored people in the townships and rural areas of South Africa.

When I came to Africa, I was surprised to experience that when I spoke, people knew how to listen very carefully. They heard every word that was said and they wanted to act upon it. This was a different experience, because I was so used to experiencing that words were not taken seriously. Elsewhere, what was said mostly went from one ear to the other. In South Africa I experienced that black people would listen to every word and act upon it. That called for extreme care when speaking. For example, when talking

1

about Waldorf education, people would wish to see how it is done. Just explaining it was not enough. They wanted to act upon the words.

In addition, we also have to develop the kind of will black South African people have. In order to associate meaningfully with the black people, one has to develop the same kind of determination never to give up in the face of obstacles, never to sway from the path one has chosen.

While the whole world has concentrated on the negative aspects of South Africa—the segregational apartheid system imposed by law upon the people—the world still has to see the essence of what black people really represent.

Long before the Europeans came to South Africa, most African communities were socially well organized and had developed remarkable cultural traditions.

There always have been strong connections to the supernatural. Knowledge of the unity of the spiritual and the natural never fell apart as it did in the dualistic perception of the Europeans.

Today, enhanced and metamorphosed by the Christian faith, religion is the deepest, most important motivating force within the majority of black people. In what other part of the world would we be able to see a theatric performance about Christ, as was presented by John Kani, the black South African playwright and actor, in *The Lion and the Lamb* in Johannesburg in 1991. Supported by three actresses, mostly acting the women in the life of Christ, he told the story of His life from the annunciation to Mary to what happened after the resurrection. This was done with utter reverence, conveying to the spellbound audience the actual reality and meaning of the life of Christ.

Originally, all indigenous peoples were holistic in their outlook and much of this is preserved to this day. The round form of their huts could stand as a symbol for the wholeness of their life experience. The interest and well-being of the family and community of which they are a part always comes before personal well-being.

As a member of the world community, Africa is not standing isolated anymore. One can expect the African continent to move toward "modern" life only if one is prepared to take full advantage of learning from the African people what has been lost in the course of evolution.

This also holds true for the international Waldorf education movement. The first Waldorf School was started in 1919 in Germany, based on Rudolf Steiner's[2] insights into the developmental phases of the human being. Since that time, this impulse has developed into a global movement with hundreds of schools all over the world. In South Africa, new enlivening and vitalization of this impulse is needed if Waldorf schools are to connect with the roots of the African experience. Failing to do so might prevent the European and African streams to merge and become one. This process can truly be realized only if people actively search for the spirit and soul of Africa and decide to come forward in the realization that "Africa we need you!"

The purpose of this book is to help bring people closer to the reality of what lives in South Africa and to show the courage displayed by people with whom we came in contact.

Instead of just describing, beginning with chapter 3, the educational initiatives resulting from the Baobab Centre's training courses, this book intends to show the character, conviction, and strength of the women behind these initiatives. They are true torchbearers. They have seen the light and they will not rest until some of that light has come to live in their communities. There are setbacks and disappointments. It takes a superhuman effort to avoid being pulled into the politics of the day and to free the educational sphere from the domination of party politics.

All the work in the different initiatives arising from activities of the Baobab Centre is done by the teachers with idealism and without expectation of great monetary reward. Yet, their families have to live, and because there are hardly any means to buy food let alone anything else, this is a great burden. But the projects develop against all odds, as though a determination of a higher order has taken over and is sustaining the spirits of all those involved.

The book also seeks to emphasize that the resources of the Western world are greatly needed to help restore the balance that was disturbed by the apartheid system and resulted in the total deprivation of millions of people.

This book attempts to document what a group of people, both Europeans and South Africans, have done since 1985, by meeting black people with the greatest reverence for their innate spirit, capacities, and goodness. They, in turn, chose to open themselves to new points of view which we offered out of our experience in working with Waldorf education. As a result, Waldorf schools in different townships and in several rural areas have sprung from the umbrella initiative, called the Centre for the Art of Living (now an Educational Trust) described in chapter 2.

In response to increasing requests for in-depth training in Waldorf education, at the end of 1991, we expanded our training courses for pre-school as well as primary school teachers, previously administered under the umbrella of the Baobab Centre, into the full-fledged activities of the Baobab Community College.

The best we can give toward restoration of a country is investment in the education of the young. This has been our initiative: to provide schools and teacher training opportunities. However, we are dependent on those people in business who trust this initiative and are willing to invest money in the children, the future of South Africa. "It is late but not too late for a New Age in Africa."

We hope what happens in South Africa will have a positive influence throughout the entire continent.

Two prophecies were told in East Africa about the white man. One warned the Kikuyu to beware
> Of strangers, who would come with
> Sticks that made fire
> And an iron snake no arrows could kill.

The other prophecy, given by a rainmaker, said:
> "A people from over the seas will come
> A people with pink cheeks and pink ears
> When they come, listen well to their words
> For they are a wise people and will bring you good."

> The first prophecy has proven true.
> The "pink cheeks" who came had eyes more for physical wealth
> Than treasures of spirit.
> But while the selfish sowing of the past
> Has led to a harvest of separation and conflict,
> The nature of the sowing can change.

> The second prophecy can still come true.
> There can still be a creative partnership based on trust,
> Respect and love,
> For that which life offers through another race.

Life has a beautiful design waiting
For Africa
For the whole world.[3]

The Baobab Community College as well as the pilot project of the Inkanyezi Waldorf Centre are located in Alexandra, a severely deprived township on the outskirts of Johannesburg, South Africa. We trust that what has been started there and is connected with the roots of Africa will be a source of inspiration and have a ripple effect into ever widening circles, as well as attract help from the wider community for its continuation and expansion.

Truus Geraets
Centre for the Art of Living
P.O. Box 2302
Rivonia 2128
South Africa
March, 1993

CHAPTER I

LIFE CIRCUMSTANCES IN SOUTH AFRICA

The Political Situation in South Africa from 1984 to 1993

What were the circumstances in which I found people living in South Africa when I moved there in 1984? Being aware of some of these situations, one will have a better understanding of why my friends and I felt so strong a need for social renewal and why we tried to help it along in whatever small way we could and why we are continuing to do so. First, however, we need to briefly describe the political background against which all this took place.

In 1984, Nelson Mandela was still in jail and the National Party was in full power, though seriously challenged by the international community. South Africa was a police state.

Under the Group Areas Act, an oppressive law of apartheid, blacks had the right to stay in the townships if they were born there, or if they had a valid reason to live there—like working for the whites outside the township. Blacks were issued passes for traveling and they were obliged to carry their passes at all times. If they were found traveling without permit, there were penalties. Thus, total control could be exercised over their mobility and lives.

Black people were allowed to own land only in the so-called "homelands," comprising just 13 percent of the total land available for 80% of the entire population.

The majority of the workforce was employed as migrant laborers who had to leave their families in the homelands, work in the mines and factories, and live in hostels in the black townships, seeing their families only after long intervals. Black women working as domestics had to leave their children in their villages and saw them perhaps once a month, at times only once a year. One can hardly fathom the hardship and suffering this brought and still brings to millions of people.

Any kind of opposition against these unjust laws was harshly suppressed. Many black leaders like Steve Biko, who spearheaded the Black Consciousness Movement, lost their lives at the hands of the police.

But, as in so many countries where totalitarian regimes were in power, the winds of change began to blow also in South Africa. The black South Africans, aided by the white fight against injustice and the world's outcry about the abuse of human rights finally found a more favorable climate. When F.W. de Klerk delivered his famous speech at the opening of parliament in February 1990, he immediately started to steer the "ship of state" in a new direction. After the release of Mandela and the unbanning of all political parties and organizations, the ice had finally broken. In the words of Christopher Fry:

> The frozen misery of centuries
> breaks, cracks, begins to move
> The thunder is the thunder of the floes
> The thaw, the flood, the upstart spring
> Thank God our Time is now.[4]

At that point, all political opposition parties and organizations, having been in exile or gone underground for decades, became legal and could reestablish themselves. A tremendous struggle for power ensued. Often through intimidation people were forced to join one or the other power bloc. Groups to the left and the right of the political center misused the situation in an attempt to increase the already existing chaos.

Although much of the unrest was incited by renegade groups, in terms of death toll the black people, again, paid the highest price. The government was heading in a new direction, but some police took sides or allowed killings to take place. At first, the winds of change brought more violence to the country than ever before. And with more political violence, the crime rates increased tremendously.

Just before Christmas of 1991, a most important historical event took place: The Conference for a Democratic South Africa (CODESA), in which 19 political parties and organizations as well as trade unions and the governments of the homelands participated in talks with the government. CODESA's aim was to begin negotiations for a new dispensation of equal rights for all South African citizens. We wonder what effect these changes will have on the socio-educational work we have been doing since 1985. We surely hope that through new trustbuilding the level of violence will gradually taper off. The expected new interim government is supposed to give special attention to the high level of violence and intimidation.

Since the opening of the Inkanyezi Children's Garden in Alexandra in 1986 (*Inkanyezi* is the Zulu word for star mentioned in chapter 5) and also of other centers in townships, the teachers had to evaluate the situation from day to day to decide whether it would be safe for the children to come to the centers. Now that a shift of power can reasonably be expected, people may refrain from continued marches and protest meetings. Time will show how effective CODESA can be. As of Christmas 1991, however, there is new hope, as expressed by the general secretary of the ANC, Cyril Ramaphosa.

> This Christmas (1991), there will be a present under everybody's Christmas tree and the name of it is CODESA.

To say "everybody's Christmas tree" is probably saying too much. Ultra-right and ultra-left groups are not prepared to participate in the negotiations and must, therefore, be considered potentially dangerous and likely to stir more violence.

One year after CODESA it was already clear that violence has not subsided, but increased instead. The attacks on trains continue week after week. The township violence—now caused by a mixture of political and criminal elements—seems hard to control. Forty years of apartheid, leaving the majority of people on the margin of existence without proper education and job skills, haunts the country and will for years to come.

The patterns of violence constantly change in strength, duration, and place, just like the weather, which can be abrupt, with violent storms and hail showers, stopping again as suddenly as they started. However, there is always this undercurrent of latent powers that, in contrast to a democratic society, never were allowed access to the usual channels for expressing themselves and of having a voice. Therefore they continue to break out in violent upheavals.

Politics in South Africa took an amazing turn when President de Klerk called for a referendum on the question: Do you support a process of negotiation? March 17, 1992, the date of the referendum, became a historical day, as voters went to the polling stations in overwhelming numbers. It was clear that here every individual voice was needed to keep the country on track toward of a negotiated settlement based on a new constitution for all South

Africans, regardless of the color of their skin.

There was only one month to prepare for this referendum. It was marked by a hectic campaign and feverish war of words. There was great uncertainty about the outcome of this whites-only event. A vote of "no" by the majority would have turned the clock back at least 40 years to the time when apartheid was introduced in South Africa. Imagine the sigh of relief among the majority of white South Africans and of the international community when a landslide decision told Mr. de Klerk that he was on the right path and that white people were prepared to include their black, colored, and Indian compatriots as full citizens.

The weeks leading up to the referendum left great violence in their wake. Once more, the black, colored, and Indian populations had to watch from the sidelines how three million whites made up their minds about the destiny of the other 27 million people in the country.

Again, a force was at work, by now known as "the third force," to make the country ungovernable. Each day brought new reports of horrific attacks on trains; numerous people were shot, attacked with long, double-edged knives used to cut grass but often used as weapons, called *pangas*, and/or thrown off moving trains, mostly between Soweto and Johannesburg. In Alexandra the beast was on the loose again with much senseless killing and an enormous increase in criminal activity, both of which mostly go hand in hand. As suddenly as the unrest started, it died down again, just one day before the date of the referendum.

After the results of the referendum were released, F.W. de Klerk thanked Providence for guiding his country to a new future. He appealed to all to see the big lines and stand in unity to make the new South Africa a reality for all. He ended with the poem by the Afrikaans poet H. A. Fagan (1889-1963) which we translate as:

> We ask your blessing, Lord, for Africa
> I gaze, and see a crowd before me,
> Zulus, Xhosa, Sotho and Shangaan,
> and I, a White one standing here.
> Many nations, yes
> United here to ask God's blessing
> on this one home, one native country
> for the Almighty put us here together
> and let us root here in South Africa.
> O Lord, bless Africa

Bless, Lord, the country,
encompassing so many nations.

May peace descend and violence subside. The southernmost tip of Africa could become a model for a peaceful multi-ethnic, multi-cultural, multi-racial country. The entire southern African region depends on such a success.

There is reason for new hope, for all of us.

Mass Migration to the Black Townships

As mentioned earlier, under the Group Areas Act, blacks were not allowed to move freely without permission. When this oppressive law was eliminated in 1991, hundreds of thousands of people left the rural areas in search of work and flocked to the townships located in proximity of the cities. As a result, the townships became totally congested. Most people cannot find work because they are unskilled and therefore join the legions of the unemployed, thereby pushing up the unemployment rate that in 1992 hovered around 50%.

Traditionally, migrant laborers working in the mines were housed in huge hostels that gradually grew into townships. Soweto, meaning South West Township, is one of them. It is located a distance away from the white urban areas. At present, Soweto has about one-and-a-half million inhabitants. With exception of those areas in which wealthier black people live, most are conglomerates of little matchbox houses. The overcrowding is so enormous that in each of those small houses an average of 14 people live.

Life is informal. Many people try to make a living by selling food from their garages or liquor from their houses, called shebeens, an English word referring to informal pubs run from people's homes in townships. The crime rate went up enormously and the most vicious gangs make the streets unsafe.

Alexandra is different from Soweto and the other townships in that people used to own their houses in Alexandra until the state disowned them and property owners became tenants against their will. That condition created enormous friction between the town councils and the inhabitants who retaliated with rent and electricity boycotts. It was one of the few means by which the apartheid system could be resisted. In turn, the town councils cut off the supply of electricity, adding to the hardship of the township dwellers. Because of the lack of income from rents and electricity, the town councils had no money to render even the most basic services to the townships, such as garbage removal. As a consequence, rubbish dumps are found everywhere in the townships. This increases the misery of already low-level hygienic conditions.

After long deliberations by the diverse councils and civic organizations, a decision was reached early in 1993 to combine the administrations of Randburg, Sandton, and Alexandra. We hope this will help our work.

Visiting people in the various townships of Alexandra, Soweto, Sharpeville, and Gugulethu (Cape Province), getting to know their ways of coping with these most difficult circumstances, seeing how inspite of these they attempt to create a wholesome life for their children, certainly enhances one's respect for them. One has to admire their courage and dignity.

CHAPTER II

IMPULSE FOR CHANGE IN THE SOCIAL AREA

Founding the Centre for the Art of Living

Coming to South Africa in 1984, my first impression was that black and white people were like oil and water, passing each other but not really mixing. Black people were living in a white society where walls, iron gates, high fences, locks and burglar bars were everywhere.

At that time there was a deep longing in the hearts of several individuals from Holland, Belgium, and South Africa to contribute something of value to the dismal social situation of fear, distrust, helplessness and exploitation in this land of apartheid. We started out by only wanting to create an opportunity for people of different color to meet and share, so that new respect could grow between them in an otherwise divided society.

In May 1985, this longing took on a more concrete form. Six of us, "the carrying group," as we called ourselves, took the initiative.

There was Cindy who had the initial talks with me. She started the Organic Village Market in Bryanston some 13 years ago. Two mornings a week the market is buzzing with people coming from near and far, selling and buying organic vegetables and craft articles. This market gives substantial support to the Waldorf School in Johannesburg.

Then there were David, a management consultant for ODISA[5] and Carol, his wife, mother of his four children, drama teacher, and arts and crafts specialist with Waldorf nursery school experience. Carol never took "no" for an answer, yet was as sensitive as anyone in leaving space for others.

There was also Janin who had come from Belgium to lecture on sociology at UNISA, the Corresponding University in Pretoria, much used by the people of South Africa including black students. When she left to study at the Centre for Social Development at

Emerson College in England, we missed her very much.

The group also included Claartje, who had 30 years of experience as a Waldorf teacher in Amsterdam and was determined to share the good things of Waldorf education with black people in Africa and I, having been associated with Waldorf education for over 30 years.

As we sat down to talk about how we could bring people together, it was clear to us that we would refrain from any kind of involvement concerning parties or politics. We saw and still see our task not in choosing sides but in building bridges, although we were and are, of course, affected by the whole political situation.

At first we thought art would be the best medium to bring people together, because art can really open spaces into which a new spirit can enter. But as more people joined our deliberations, all having the desire to do something meaningful in the country's situation, ideas took a different form. We realized our goal had to be higher than merely involving people through art. A wider scale had to be encompassed. We needed to create an environment where the "art of living" could be practiced. Social renewal in South Africa was the goal to which we wanted to contribute. Thus, as the first step toward that goal we decided to inaugurate a facility and call it the Centre for the Art of Living.

A presumptuous name, it may seem. What does it do for the social situation? How can people be bothered with the art of living when they have nothing to eat and no roof above their head? Many people shook their heads when they heard the name for the first time. It was a concept totally alien to them.

Different explanations about the art of living were given us. One person said the art of living was not so difficult but the problem was the art of living *together.*

Several months after we had chosen the name and were hosting our first conference (on social renewal in November 1985), one of the participants of the conference, Mr. Robert Mazibuko from the Africa Tree Centre in Natal, told us he was taken by the name. He said:

> Yes, all my life—and now I am 80 years old—I have searched for a name of what I actually have been pursuing. This is it, this is the name for it: The Art of Living.

And later at Christmastime, a teenager who spent two weeks with us during our Christmas Rainbow Programme, saw it this way. In her short essay at the end of the program she wrote that here she learned the art of *making* a living, as she had learned to make candles, to make a leather purse, to make bread and pizza, and so on. We had not thought of such an explanation. Yet, it was actually quite accurate. Giving a name like that had and has its obligations. Once given, we had to fill the name with life.

The Centre's Task of Providing an Overall Perspective

After the choice of name was made in May 1985, we had to ask ourselves: What form should our work take? How should we be organized? In trying to write our founding document we had to formulate our aims and goals. We stated them in very general terms.

At that time we did not yet know what specific applications would be called for by outside circumstances. For example, we did not anticipate the need for specific work in education until the school crisis occurred in the following winter. But when it occurred, we inaugurated the Baobab Centre for Teacher Enrichment under the umbrella of the Centre for the Art of Living.

And when it became necessary to convince black teachers that Waldorf education was not only a white luxury, the Inkanyezi Rainbow Project was born. Thus, as time went on, more and more projects arose under the umbrella of the Centre for the Art of Living.

Often we were so involved in what our friend Jill would call "brick-and-mortar" projects that we wondered what the reality of the umbrella organization was. But then she would say: "People will be interested in you because of your big concept of social renewal."

Another confirmation of this initiative was that we received funding specifically for the consolidation of the Centre for the Art of Living.

From the beginning we had the continuing challenge of keeping the original impulse alive. This held true not only for each individual but also for the group as such, regardless of who belonged to it. Without a common vision or goal we cannot really cooperate with each other. Therefore we need to spend time together asking ourselves: Why are we doing this? What direction should our work be taking? What do we really mean by social renewal? How do we see the development of the individual in connection with the development of society as a whole? Also, what

14

is happening in the world around us? Can we read what wants to manifest? In short, by studying together and exchanging our experiences we have and are still trying to become more aware of what we really are doing and thereby heighten our responsibility of how we should develop and improve the work.

Another way of staying alive in the process is through the medium of art. The real artist looks at his work from a distance. The good musician not only produces but listens to his music as well. Likewise, throughout the process, we are trying to become better "life artists" ourselves. We must be able to step back from our projects in order to see the whole again and allow for unexpected developments to take place. We have to be realistic and practical without losing ourselves in the details of the projects. Basically, then, those of us who keep the Centre for the Art of Living going had and have the task of providing an overall perspective.

The Centre's Task of Raising Funds

Concerning physical maintenance, the Centre itself did not

require much. It needed legal status as an organization, it needed a postal address. In the very beginning, the rent of the house we were using for the different activities as well as for the office was donated by the landlady. After that period, the homes of the various members served as base of activity until 1992 when we were finally able to move into our own facility.

For the first six months in 1985 we worked with an absolute minimum of costs. Only one of the different people involved with the project earned some money. Whatever we had in equipment was given us. We knew we had to start small and could hope for support only from our closest friends until we had proven ourselves.

As individual projects started, we began to need funds. The first person beyond the close circle of friends supporting our work was Mr. King, Manager of the Anglo-American and De Beers Chairman's Fund. Janin was still with us at that time and able to go to the first interview explaining our initiative to Mr. King.

When we needed support for Inkanyezi Children's Garden, a close friend of the Centre for the Art of Living helped us financially as all creches and nursery schools depend on private funding. DET (Department of Education and Training, instated for the education of black people only) does not subsidize nursery schools or private schools.

Having to raise funds meant we had to learn how to do that. Different organizations have different attitudes about giving money. Some give a small amount to each organization requesting help. Clearly, they want to have a good name in the community at large. Others, such as embassies, are interested only in capital investment. Then there are others who will give a one-time gift for equipment, or they will give only if one can draw up a three to five year development program for the project. Other big companies take care of their own employees first, giving low-interest loans for housing or education of the children. Then there are other companies that will give money only in combination with manpower and expertise. One such company in Switzerland helped with experts as well as with machinery for working with leather and wood. In such cases we have to find out first if such expertise will fit in with our overall intentions, as we must keep our training basic and attuned to our social efforts.

Many of the potential sponsors respond positively to our invitation of visiting our nursery school and workshops. For follow-up we give regular reports so that donors can follow what is happening with their money. Since money also represents power and we must stay clear from any political influencing that could be connected with donations, we appreciate a distribution of donors. What we most appreciate is money given freely out of sincere interest and understanding of our projects.

Although economic life is not known for altruism and brotherhood, big companies are becoming more aware of their social influence and responsibility. Words like "social concern," used by an African bank, "social responsibility" projects, or names like "The Quality of Life Fund," indicate that. One big oil company states it thusly:

> But the responsibility for creating an acceptable quality of life, which is the birthright of every South African, is not the responsibility of the government alone but of every South African, including the corporate citizens.

And in the words of an insurance company:

> The future of our company is intimately tied up with the future welfare and prosperity of the country and its people, so it is in our own material interest to promote the country's welfare and progress.

In the beginning, because of the connections our group members had overseas, two thirds of the monies necessary for the school and workshops came from abroad.

While fundraising in the Netherlands, I found some fund managers extremely well informed about the situation in South Africa and Alexandra in particular. They asked detailed questions and made pertinent comments. I was also amazed to find a booklet by the Information Service of the Dutch Government listing all the organizations that have anything to do with third-world countries. This was helpful information.

As was probably to be expected, some of our donors from overseas suggested that more local funds be tapped. South Africa is not a poor country. Unfortunately, the need for help is so overwhelming that those who are willing to help are overtaxed. One South African company told us they are already involved in helping three other nursery schools in Alexandra and they would have to spread their monies more equally over the whole country than spending it just in one township.

As time went on, additional avenues of support opened up. They will be mentioned in connection with those projects. Since

1991, the Centre for the Art of Living is registered as an Educational Trust, thus officially fulfilling its function of being an umbrella organization not only for ideas and goals, but also for chaneling monetary support to the increased number of initiatives that have arisen under its sponsorship. But let us return to the specific work begun after the Centre for the Art of Living was formed.

First Projects Arising from the Centre for the Art of Living

What were the specific developments after the Centre was founded in May 1985? Three months after the initial talks, Cindy offered space free of charge in her big house in Rivonia, a northern suburb of Johannesburg. Having space available for activities of the Centre, we could begin to implement our idea of building bridges by bringing people together.

We had assumed it would be simple to bring people of different cultures and races together. However, we did not consider that the house was rather far away, especially for people from Soweto and also from the other townships, nor how serious the transportation problem was for black people, few of whom have their own car. Most must rely on the small minibuses, the taxis, as they are called, and the public buses. Black people would be interested to come to the Centre for training, if a comprehensive training package could be offered for a week. But to come only for the sake of meeting other people or to do something such as attending a lecture or painting class, was not enough.

So we tried to adjust the program and got some interesting and well-attended courses and talks going, such as a course on African mythology, a lecture on the Southern hemisphere, a course on world evolution, and on personal development. ODISA held a course on developing social skills. Also, different art courses were held with good attendance. Sometimes we celebrated festivals together with a number of people. Yet, it became clear that what we had to offer was not yet solid enough.

The Conference on Social Renewal

After the founding of the Centre for the Art of Living, Christine, a former Waldorf teacher connected with the Centre, started to plan a conference on social renewal on a weekend in November 1985.

On that weekend, nine black people from townships near Johannesburg as well as from rural Natal came to meet with 15 white people to exchange views on the situation in the country and what could be done about it. This was where the real start of the Centre for the Art of Living occurred.

That weekend we learned much from each other. I received my first insight into life in Soweto when I listened to Jada and Jabu who live there. Ian, at that time our accountant, who was working closely with them, described the endless frustration black people experience trying to achieve anything through the bureaucratic system. It is already difficult enough for white people, but for black people, who often cannot speak English or Afrikaans, may even be illiterate, and have to deal with oppressive laws, the hurdles are almost insurmountable. Nevertheless, people refuse to give up and continue to pursue their objectives.

In addition, the white people were eager to hear from the black people about their beliefs, traditions and mythology, and how they combine these with the Western way of life. On that weekend we heard the story of a very successful black businessman who bought himself a Mercedes. He drove it straight from the dealer to the graveyard where his mother was buried, for her to see it, but specially to bless it, so that no harm would befall him or the car. This story met with understanding from the white people present. We did not just react with a condescending "Oh, well, ancestor worship," as out of the philosophy we embraced, we were equally convinced that the dead are still alive and can guide the living, if we are open to it. The idea of having a car blessed in the graveyard was unexpected additional information.

The black participants, on the other hand, found the underlying aspects of each field of work presented by the white people very revealing. The white participants had different occupational backgrounds, but most of them shared a spiritual outlook on man and the world derived from Rudolf Steiner's work. They shared their life experience in the areas of medicine, art, pharmacy, biodynamic agriculture, organizational consulting, and Waldorf education. One person was working with Operation Hunger[6]. Helene McDougall had years of experience of initiating projects in the rural communities around Himeville, Natal.

However, it was education that mainly fascinated the black participants. Because of the crisis in education, they were very eager to listen to new concepts, especially as the concept of

Waldorf education, in their words, "seemed to have a heart." When they heard we were planning to bring children of different races together for two weeks during the Christmas holidays, they were ready to send us as many children as we possibly could handle. But they also asked us what we could do for them in the long run. Were we prepared to set up a school in Rivonia? Could we possibly train teachers and then start with three classes, letting the school grow year by year? We realized that the black initiative takers had to live day by day with the urgency of the situation, but at that time we felt that we could not take on the huge responsibility.

In the end, our friends started their school with some 160 pupils without us. The school went through many upheavals, but it was remarkable that they were able to set up a private boarding school outside Soweto in only a few months.

The whole experience was a testing ground that overwhelmed us in its intensity and urgency. Yet, the idea for the St. Ansgars school was born that very weekend and during the many meetings and discussions we had after that it was possible to form a picture of the school.

The black people came away from the weekend with the feeling that their total reality had been embraced, their traditions and magic, as well as their integration into modern society. In the past, most missionaries had made them reject their traditions, but the initiative group just wanted to share the best of the cultures and achievements of the Western world, while being open to the African cultures and way of life, knowing that much could be learned from these. Then and there we realized the need to assimilate and accept their otherness fully, because we were convinced that the black people could not have a future as long as their past was denied them. We also had to learn that most black people have a great distrust of words but when their hearts can feel what one wishes to convey, they insist on putting it into practice. All participants of this Conference on Social Renewal came away with a feeling of social renewal in themselves, that slowly started to take shape in actual deeds of social renewal.

The Christmas Rainbow Programme

In December 1985, the school boycott was in full swing. We had planned an arts and crafts program with children of different backgrounds and races as a two-week happening. Because of the difficulty and cost of transportation, the 20 black children all had to stay overnight with us. Quickly, we had to borrow mattresses and blankets and find large cooking pots. But then we were ready to receive them: 14 youngsters from Soweto and six from a squatter camp not far from Soweto. Squatters was the name given to people who came from the rural areas to the townships taking possession of vacant land where they erected makeshift dwellings mostly consisting of poles and corrugated metal or cardboard and plastic sheeting.

Many white children came to the Christmas Rainbow Programme but only for certain classes. Then they went home for the night.

One of the first things we encountered was a white child asking for the special toilet for the white children. Of course, there was none. The child was in a great dilemma what to do about it, because it could not possibly use a toilet that was also used by black children! But on the whole, the interaction was very good and without problems. They were just children, having a good time. In fact, the black children helped us greatly by taking on two very difficult white children, who actually were too young and hard to handle.

The black children from Soweto had one special fun game they called "roadblocks." They would slide down the brick banister of the outside staircase and something or somebody had to obstruct the flow of children sliding down. Thus they played out in their games the things they experienced in the township. At that time, roadblocks were a frequent occurrence in the townships where the soldiers put up sand barriers in such a way that cars and taxis had to drive a slow slalom between them. That way the soldiers, manning the roadblocks, or the police could easily stop the cars and search for illegal weapons or anything or anyone deemed "illegal."

The squatter children were quite different. It was immediately clear from their faces that they had endured much hardship. We heard they had been moving around from one place to the next, always being told they were not welcome. At the Rainbow Programme they made the discovery that not all whites hate them. One of the squatter children wrote at the end of her stay in a little essay about her holiday at the Centre for the Art of Living: "Here, people are not mean and horrible to you. Here, they just want to be friends with you." It touched our hearts deeply.

The boys were a group of their own, not used to doing things together with the girls. At one point we were afraid of losing their interest altogether, but then we discovered how the art of baking bread appealed to them. First, they could use their physical strength in kneading the dough, while later on they had a great feeling of satisfaction and pride when the loaves, all marked with their own initials, would be on the tables, ready for everyone to eat. In the same way we made pizza together, something they had only seen on television but never eaten. Whatever we were going to eat, the children would cook or bake: chocolate pudding, pumpkin soup, speculatius cookies, whatever. I was amazed that they had no problem eating this food, which was very different from their ordinary diet.

We found the black children very keen to learn; they really were achievers. Every morning we began by practicing with them a Christmas play by Selma Lagerlöf. The children worked very hard on learning their lines and in the end performed a lovely play for all the parents and invited guests. That really was a wonderful afternoon, culminating when all 70 people, children and adults alike, did eurythmy[7] together outside on the lawn. The children proudly took home their self-made candles, tie-and-dye cloths, transparencies, and leather purses.

Many weeks later we heard that one of the squatter children, a chronic bedwetter, had stopped wetting his bed after the positive experience of the Christmas Rainbow Programme.

Six years later, I met Mavis, one of the children who participated in the Rainbow Programme. The two weeks in Rivonia made a lasting impression on her. When I met her again, she was about 18 years of age and preparing for her matric (matriculation) exam. Passing this exam entitles the student to apply for university enrollment. Mavis was intending to become a teacher and wanted to teach in a school where learning can be a joy. Six years earlier, Mavis was still a child, but when we met her again, we could talk with her and explain that the whole Rainbow Programme was based on the Waldorf education impulse, in which arts and crafts play such an important role in child development.

CHAPTER III

IMPULSE FOR CHANGE IN THE EDUCATIONAL AREA

The Educational Scene in South Africa 1985-1986

In December 1985 the educational world in South Africa was in turmoil. The school boycotts in the townships had been going on for 18 months. Children were losing out on any consistent education. Already in 1976 with the uprising in Soweto, the youth had violently objected to the inferior Bantu education[8] and to the fact that they were being taught in Afrikaans, language of the oppressor.

Ever since that time, any stability of schooling was absent and a full-blown education crisis began to establish itself. Any child who might still intend going to school was put under enormous pressure. The students in charge of the boycott did not intend to give in unless their demands were met. By 1985 these demands expanded to include political issues. Teachers and inspectors were molested by the students for being lackeys of the government, school buildings were vandalized, and a minority of the most militant pupils intimidated others and prevented them from attending lessons.

Education had been used for political purposes and thereby lost its integrity. For this reason it was inevitable that a crisis would come. For years, young people were made to fit into a tight mold with inadequate means and by totally unqualified teachers. The young people were crying for something different. But what was it they were really searching for? The whole subject matter is very complex and many books and essays have been written on the theme.

In the final analysis it was clear that the young people who participated in the school boycott hurt themselves most by missing years of schooling. In the end they would be the losers, forfeiting any opportunity to uplift the lot of their own people. Clearly, something needed to be done.

The children of the Sowetan friends participating in our Conference of Social Renewal in November 1985 suffered the same fate as the other black children. For this reason we had planned the Christmas Rainbow Programme for them. We realized that this was not enough. Education as such needed to be invigorated beginning with the training of teachers. This realization prompted us to action.

Founding the Baobab Centre for Teacher Enrichment

When we began to realize that something needed to be done to enliven the education of black children and to enrich the training of their teachers, we knew we needed a vehicle to do so. For this purpose we founded the Baobab Centre for Teacher Enrichment under the umbrella of the Centre for the Art of Living. This occurred at the beginning of 1986. It enabled us to offer workshops and courses for teachers.

Education had become a wasteland, dry, and abstract; it had been pulled into the political battlefield and was urgently in need of a new impulse, a new direction, born out of true insights into the nature of the child. The Baobab trainers believed that a new spiritual outlook regarding education could become a fountain of renewed life in this most important area: the introduction of the child to the world, while letting the world benefit from the fresh spiritual impulses coming from the child. This, for us, is education.

The word *education* itself was felt to be totally inadequate for what we wanted to promote. Education had become synonymous with passivity, dependence, timidity, confinement, uniformity, consumerism. We wanted to use the terms nonformal education or education for life.

We realized that much depends on teachers' training to achieve a more lively, comprehensive, and holistic education for children. Future teachers must be challenged to work as much on their own development as to acquire understanding of the children in their care. They also are to develop an insight into the ways society operates or should not operate. They are to become as skilled in artistic and craft work as in academic subjects. They are to develop skills in communication and conflict solving and need to understand the value of teamwork. Teachers also have to learn about the administrative and financial sides of the school. In student teachers the feeling would have to be awakened of the deep responsibility for each individual child in context with the healthy social life of the whole school. At the same time, openness to the world, the environment, and humanity as a whole must be fostered. An awesome task, indeed!

Why We Chose the Name Baobab Centre

"We are the roots of a big tree," wrote the black South African poet Jeremiah Phechudi. This statement has a deeper meaning and so does the name we chose for the educational impulse springing from the Centre for the Art of Living. The Baobab tree, our symbol, is a truly African symbol. It can become so old—up to 5000 years— and yet be so young. It is a symbol of life, as every part of this tree can be used either for food and medicine, or for making ropes,

baskets, and fiber cloth. The Baobab tree is like a fountain in the dry landscape of the savannah because 16% of the tree consist of water. In times of drought, elephants seek out the trees to strip off the bark and gouge out the water fibers, leaving the trees with gaping holes. But the trees have a remarkable capacity for generating new bark and thus for recovering.

There is a legend in which the Baobab tree is called the upside-down tree, because of its odd shape and its branches that look like roots rather than real branches. Strangely enough, young Baobab trees do not yet look like that at all. They do not have the big, swollen trunk but develop into their final shape only gradually. It takes about 40 years for the young tree to start changing its shape and resembling the mother tree. Small wonder, then, that the Baobab tree is venerated and the subject of many tales and legends.[9]

Seeing the tree in the landscapes of northern Transvaal, standing like a lonely giant, benignly overlooking all the other trees and bushes in those vast expanses, is a breathtaking sight, indeed. Farther north, in Zimbabwe, Baobab trees are more frequent and one can even see them growing in clusters. They are awe-inspiring relics of the past.

What most fascinated the group willing to be Baobab trainers was the fact that the Baobab tree can be compared to a fountain of life in a desert. For this reason it most aptly represented what we tried to achieve with the Baobab Centre for Teacher Enrichment.

The Beginnings of Teacher Enrichment Training

Beginning in 1986, for more than two years, we conducted regular courses for nursery and primary school teachers at the Funda Centre in Soweto, an adult education center for blacks established in 1984 by the private sector in Soweto. The Director of the Section for Continued Teacher Training, Dr. Franz Auerbach, was very understanding and supportive of what we were trying to bring. He was excited about the fact that we placed great emphasis on teaching methods as well as on self-development of the teacher through artistic training. This is almost completely missing in official teacher training courses.

Franz Auerbach noticed that the teachers continued to come and in general the number of participants was increasing rather than diminishing. Considering how tough the lives of these teachers were, this was remarkable.

Teachers in the townships are mostly women. Besides long teaching days with very large classes of 50 to 60 pupils each, the teachers have to do all the cooking, cleaning, and washing for the whole family when they get home. For this reason it is a sacrifice for them to attend extra training courses. In addition, our courses were not for the purpose of increasing qualifications and correspondingly salaries. For that reason is was even more remarkable that the teachers kept coming.

The Waldorf approach was what appealed to the teachers. They often applied in their classrooms what they had learned during the courses. Later on they would report how it had worked out for them. We showed them how even with the tight timetable given by the DET they actually could work faster and better with the children by enlivening the teaching of different subjects with arts, crafts, and drama.

In the training courses the teachers participated in painting, drawing, and eurythmy. They were engaged in story telling with table puppets and shadow theater. They started to realize for themselves that learning could become a real pleasure. Above all, the teachers started feeling confident they would be able to cope with the very difficult educational environment. But they also developed a new sense of wonder for the being of the child, as they learned more about the phases of child development.

The Conference on Education in 1986

Not only black children were unhappy with their education, many white children were unhappy too. Thus we were not surprised when we were asked to organize another weekend conference, but this time specifically on the whole issue of education. We decided to invite a number of teachers and educators to this conference for an exchange of views about the issues of education. This conference took place in February 1986.

At the beginning of the conference we immediately pointed out that education was in a turmoil worldwide. While young people come into the world with new realities, new visions, the older generation very seldom has the flexibility or the wish to adapt to the new impulses. Children have to fit into the mold of the existing society rather than society allowing itself to be renewed by what lives as a positive will in the young people. This is a problem worldwide and not only in South Africa.

If one assumes that a child comes into this world as an unwritten sheet of paper, it is natural to think that the child can only develop by receiving all the experience, knowledge, and information about the world from the older generation. However, the moment one sees the child as a being with innate capabilities and impulses of its own, that must be given space to develop and grow, a process of continued renewal can take place rather than stagnation and a fixed repetition of the same.

For children to grow into adults who can make positive contributions to the world out of a clear sense of self-identity, it is necessary that they are not only overwhelmed with information but are engaged with their feeling and receive stimulation for their will. The ideal is that as a result of the full involvement of their whole being in school, children develop their thinking, feeling, and willing towards full responsibility as adults.

The educational conference was attended by teachers black and white, teachers from the townships as well as from rural areas. Because the atmosphere was one of openness, the black teachers freely and fully expressed their feelings and experiences. Some could tell how the use of Waldorf concepts in their classes changed their teaching.

One teacher in a primary school in Soweto, who had received some of our training, actually started to introduce a whole new way of teaching in her class, with the result that parents came to ask what actually happened in her class. They were astounded that their children did not want to miss even one day of school anymore.

Other teachers expressed their deep frustration at being wedged in, or rather torn apart by the demands of the inspectors and the wishes of the pupils. They could see the reality of the children's demands, yet were in fear of losing their jobs.

This topic, fear of losing one's job, was addressed by Dr. Franz Auerbach. He stressed that fear would have to be lifted from the teachers; fear of the hierarchy of the DET on the one hand and fear of the angry and politicized students on the other.

Jack Moens, President of the Dutch Waldorf Association, an organization of 70 Waldorf schools in Holland, who had come to visit with us, made the point that not only in South Africa do we deal with a multicultural problem. Throughout the world we are confronted with this reality more and more. Even more problematic than a multicultural situation is the situation of children belonging to different major world religions. As teachers, we have to learn the skills of working with each other's backgrounds and how to handle a great diversity of children. Teachers as well as pupils need to learn new social skills for the future. For the teachers this must be part of their training in teachers' colleges.

The basis of the Waldorf school impulse lies in the realm of social healing. Through such a school, new impulses can flow back into the community in which teachers, children, and parents recognize their interdependence and start to work toward cooperation and mutual support.

At the end of the discussions, Guy Wertheim-Aymes, director of Pharma Natura, a pharmaceutical factory for homeopathic and Weleda medicines located in Wynberg, adjacent to Alexandra township, made the suggestion for us to start a school based on Waldorf school principles in Alexandra. He was willing to assist us financially even more than he had already, if we could get going with this suggestion.

Guy Wertheim-Aymes' offer gave us the opportunity to start realizing our vision. But how to go about it? Without full cooperation of the people in the township we could not be successful. The important thing was to train black people in such a way that they would understand the basic ideas behind Waldorf education, yet develop the confidence, insight, and flexibility to develop these ideas further in connection with the specific needs of the children they would be dealing with.

The school initiative would have to start with a nursery school. There is a chronic shortage of places for children of preschool age. In 1988, there were 15,000 such children in Alexandra and only about 500 children found places in the five nursery schools. As these nursery schools work mostly with private funding, they struggle from year to year, wondering if they will survive the next year. And before we could start a nursery school, we would have to train the teachers for the nursery school first. Thus we came round circle to the need for teacher training.

What is Waldorf Education?

For us, Waldorf education means universality, as it is based on the developmental stages of the human being as such, independent of race, creed or country. Waldorf schools all over the world are for all children and are successfully operating with Maori children in New Zealand, with Japanese children, and with children of different religious beliefs all in one school.

From the start of the first Waldorf School in Stuttgart, Germany, in 1919, the school had a strong practical orientation in combination with development of the mind. There is also much emphasis on artistic expression. Being a Waldorf teacher is a big challenge, as the teacher must present each subject in an artistic way. There is no easy reading from a book or a dry summing up of facts. Also learning by rote should be replaced by learning out of pure interest. The teacher must make the subject material alive for the student and, therefore, needs to prepare himself or herself very well. It mainly depends on the teacher's effort and preparation how enthusiasm and energy carry the experience of the subject to the child. This way, students are enlivened and motivated to find out more about the world by themselves. Students leaving the school after 12 years should be ready not only for society but for life in general. They should have learned the art of living.

We had heard that so many young black people who managed under great duress to obtain a matric certificate, thinking this would be the key to a better position in life, were still unable to obtain a job. Clearly, students need more than information and knowledge to make a success of their lives. We knew that through Waldorf education the pupils would gain the necessary self-confidence and ability to think for themselves so as to form sound judgments about life. The aim of Waldorf education is that children grow into responsible people who later on will be able to make an active contribution to society, transforming it according to their youthful, yet responsible insights.

Enrichment Courses and Workshops for Teachers

As time went on, several teachers experienced in Waldorf school methods provided courses and workshops directly under the auspices of the Boabab Centre. Carol, who—in addition to having many other skills—had been a nursery school teacher, concentrated more on the training of child-minders and nursery school teachers, while Claartje and Maxine, and later also Eric and Martin, used their experience as Waldorf teachers in the training of teachers.

The initial courses held after the founding of the Baobab

Centre in 1986 were indeed enrichment courses, not yet full-time training courses. Yet, the enthusiasm of the participants was such that whatever they had learned, they put into practice.

Mirriam, about whom more is written in chapter 9, attended some of our courses at the Funda Centre in Soweto in 1986-1987. She was the first to understand the depths of the concept of Waldorf education and the impact it could have on the lives of individual children as well as on the educational scene in general. She immediately bought the book *Education towards Freedom,* [10] in which the whole of Waldorf education, from nursery school to high school, is presented. The book is beautifully illustrated with work done by children, showing each developmental stage throughout the years.

In 1987, Mirriam worked as a teacher in a DET school in Soweto. She described her contact with Waldorf education:

> It was a real eye-opener for me to learn seeing the child in a completely different perspective, from how I used to look at it. Now I learned to see that the child is not only an information gatherer, but an individual with his own innate capacities and that one should give the child the opportunity to express himself. And that by doing so, I myself could learn from each child anew.

As people from the Baobab Centre shared their experiences in Waldorf education with course and workshop participants, the latter were exposed to new ideas. Waldorf education is child-centered in that the phases of the child's development are considered at every stage of the learning process.

People who participated in the workshops for nursery school teachers and child-minders learned about these developmental stages beginning at birth and even before birth. The primary school teachers, too, learned to see the vital importance of the first years of a child's life on earth.

Carol was able to present the incarnation of the human being in a most artistic way, always anew and always showing the incarnation process of the soul and spirit of the child into the body. This, more than anything else, fascinated those attending the courses.

Inner Development of the Teacher

One feature highly valued by the participants of the courses and of

31

the Education Conference in February 1986 was the attention given the development of the teacher. Franz Auerbach from the Funda Centre in Soweto, where we conducted many courses, wrote to us: "I have been most interested to note that the content of your courses influences both methods and teacher attitudes." What he called teacher attitudes, we called inner development.

At the time of all this training activity, teachers in the DET schools were squeezed on the one hand by the demands of the pupils (the comrades) who wanted to free education from government domination and on the other by the teachers who did not want to lose their jobs. Teachers lived in constant fear for their lives and jobs from both sides of the spectrum—the pupils on the one hand and the inspectors, backed by the whole hierarchical structure of the DET, on the other. The teachers had to start realizing that they were the most important players in the educational field. If they developed themselves into creative educators, full of initiative and self-confidence, they could help turn the situation around. The teachers attending our courses felt they had come across a new way of empowering themselves. Many came forward, expressing the wish to see this type of school also in their townships or rural villages.

Taking several teachers to Michael Mount Waldorf School (established since 1960) in Bryanston near Johannesburg in 1986 made them feel discouraged, as they could not fathom having such a fancy school in the township. Our task was to show them that this kind of education depends much more on the attitude of the teachers toward the pupils and themselves than on the outward structures and educational equipment. The feedback from the people at the Education Conference and from those we took to the Michael Mount Waldorf School helped us with the decision to start a school initiative in Alexandra.

CHAPTER IV

THE SITUATION IN ALEXANDRA TOWNSHIP

Alexandra Township 1963-1986

In order to gain an understanding of the situation in Alexandra, one must go back in history. Since 1963, Alexandra was not supposed to exist. Before that time it was the only township where black people could own land, "Freehold Land," as it was called.

But the government passed a death sentence on Alexandra, when it decided that Alexandra was to become a hostel city for some 80,000 migrant workers, men and women who, without their families, would have to live in separate blocks of high-rise flats and provide cheap labor for the neighboring white suburbs.

The Bantu Resettlement Board started to relocate scores of people. In one year almost 45,000 people were moved to other townships. The forced removals went on until 1983, when all the land had been expropriated. But then the original inhabitants—at least what was left of them—began to organize themselves and fight the population removals. The Alexandra Residents Committee was so successful that in 1983 all hostel development was finally terminated.

For 20 years, no development had taken place except for the most urgent repairs. The township had completely fallen into a state of neglect and decay. During the "six-day war" in 1986, streets were dug up, buildings smashed and burned, all of which added a war-torn image to this already run-down place. Alexandra had no sewage system, no electricity, only a few telephones and one water faucet for every block of seven or eight houses. When one goes there for the first time, one is overwhelmed by the stench, something the people of the township have to live with every day. Groups of 20 to 30 women are constantly trying to keep Alexandra clean, but it is an absolutely hopeless undertaking.

34

At the time the Boabab Centre was founded in 1986, Alexandra had about 100,000 inhabitants. It was much smaller than Soweto. Because of its location close to the richest suburb of Johannesburg, much attention from the private sector and the government was to go into upgrading the township. Alexandra was called the Dark City, yet it had a reputation for bringing forth many of the famous black writers, musicians, and statesmen.

With its history of total neglect of the people, of people having to give way to inhuman ways of manhandling and the most appalling living conditions, one must ask, how was it at all possible that the small group of original inhabitants left in this sizable town still had the inner fibre and energy to bounce back and fight for their right to exist as a community? There is great nobility among the core community of Alexandra.

Because of the enormous housing shortage for black people all over South Africa and the influx of many blacks from the neighboring states, a whole new population has come into being in Alexandra. These are the people who built themselves temporary shacks. They are the strangers in Alexandra. With unemployment in 1986 at 45%, one must expect a high crime rate, and we experience crime on a regular basis.

During seven months in our nursery school (opened in July 1987 and described in chapter 5) we had four break-ins. The last time we were fortunate to get practically everything back. But at other times we were not so fortunate. Insurance companies won't give insurance in Alexandra. Another problem is that most delivery companies refuse to deliver in Alexandra.

When Sue parked her car for a few moments outside the store to buy some bread for the doll makers (described in chapter 6), her car was stolen. But the old people of Itlhokomeleng Old People's Home were so outraged that this should happen to someone trying to do something worthwhile for their own people, they went on foot to search through the whole township. They found the car and told the young people who had stolen it that they should be ashamed of themselves and that they better give it back. One can count it a miracle that the old people were so outraged and thereby so courageous that they convinced the young people that they should give the car back. They did.

At the beginning of 1987, the government made the decision

that Alexandra Township should stay and be upgraded. Big renovation plans were made, of which a small part has been realized. Ramshackle huts still lean against houses that are in good condition. In each open space, squatters have put up their illegal dwellings with cardboard signs reading: "Keep out! Mafia controlled!" Between the odd combination of old and new, of highrise flats and low houses and huts, animals are roaming free: cows, horses, and numerous goats. Skinny dogs, together with chickens and cows, feed off the garbage heaps.

In 1987 and 1988, the roads were still broken up for installation of the sewage system—at long last—as well as cables for electricity and telephones. Although the whole township was in constant upheaval, the people have been very cooperative and there were no incidents of sabotage.

By 1993, the population had increased from 100,000 to 270,000 because of the tremendous influx of homeless people, as the squatters were called since 1992. It is almost impossible to cope with such a situation.

Many people, black and white alike, feel that Alexandra is a very special place. It is known as the mother township, as all the other townships, Tembisa, Soweto, etc. have sprung from Alexandra. Steven Burger, the administrator of Alexandra, who has been involved in the administration of different townships, also feels that Alexandra has a tremendous potential. There is an exceptional number of outstanding community leaders on whom the moral fibre of the township rests.

In 1988, Mr. Burger launched a work creation drive, inviting some 160 business people to help find ways of tackling the enormous unemployment problem by creating more training opportunities, and promoting home industries and markets to sell the products so that people can become self-employed in a small but real way. A shoeshine and carwash project have been started. We linked up with this project, called "Progress Through Employment" and have exhibited the articles made in our workshops (described in chapter 6) as well as provided shoe polishing brushes to the shoe shiners that were made in our sheepskin/leather workshop.

There are wonderful people in the township—very courageous people—who live with the turbulence and pressure from day to day. These people have a great impact on upholding standards of decency and service to the community.

With practically no help from the outside, the inhabitants of the township were left to their own devices and depended on mutual support. They set up several feeding programs not only for the old people but also for the unemployed. These programs were often launched from a private kitchen but then grew to such dimensions that help had to be sought either in form of monthly donations or donations of foodstuffs.

Very outstanding in its service to the Alexandra community has always been the Alexandra Taxi Association, which responds to every call from persons in urgent need of transport to or from a hospital. There are also funeral homes that have buried people for no charge.

It would, of course, be impossible to list all those organizations and individuals without whom life in the township would completely disintegrate. The people are united in their struggle and this gives them strength. It is their dignity that makes them accomplish what is almost impossible.

Helping the Youngsters

Some school principals have watched over their pupils like fathers, making sure they continued with their education beyond primary school and even beyond high school. When I asked Vielwa, our Zulu teacher, why Alexandra has such an attraction for so many people, white and black alike, she told me that Alexandra has been the birthplace of many talented and well-known leaders such as politicians and famous musicians. She is also helping many young people who were stranded in their education because of lack of funds. She helped many students out of her own pocket, but to help all the young people coming to her for help is simply beyond her capacity.

When one sees the overcrowded conditions of up to five families living in one house, meaning one family per room, it is clear that students cannot properly study at home, and it would be best for them to go to a boarding school where library facilities are available and supervision with homework. Because there is so much hooliganism in the township, it is especially important for boys to be away from the temptations and intimidations of township life.

It takes only R 700 (700 rand equal approximately 210 U.S. dollars) to send one student to a high school or trade school for a year. A much better solution, according to Vielwa, is to send the young people to multiracial, integrated schools or boarding schools. There they not only study for diplomas and certificates, but also learn skills for life by mixing with children from completely different cultures and backgrounds. Such boarding schools cost three times as much as other schools, but they would be preferred as they affect the whole personality in a positive way.

The book *Kaffir Boy*[11], written by a young man who grew up in Alexandra, paints a horrific picture of what life in this township is all about. Is there hope for Alexandra? Is there hope for South Africa? The old people are very tired of the long struggle for survival. But many more young children will now get a chance for a higher education. This is one of the means of change. It may go slowly but it is moving in a new direction. The wind of change is blowing and nobody can resist change.

Shortly after the Christmas Rainbow Programme in 1985, when the general situation in South Africa and in Alexandra specifically was still very bleak, we attended a meeting where businessmen and community leaders of Alexandra explored the real needs of Alexandra and how they could be of help. The discussion came to a standstill when it was realized that whatever they did, be it start an orchestra, grow gardens, or build buildings, nothing would work unless the question of education was handled. The youth held power in their hands and could and would destroy any initiative if they did not support it.

One of us then spoke of our vision of a project in Alexandra: a small nursery school raying out like a sun into the community, whose rays would be workshops including the community, young and old, in learning skills and making things for the nursery school.

It was a holistic picture that elicited an excited response from a big, heavy-set man, who jumped up from his seat on the other side of the conference table and spoke the words that would carry us along with so much encouragement: "Now I see light again." He immediately wanted to exchange telephone numbers with us so that he could contact us later.

In the course of time we learned that this man was a high school principal and recognized community leader. Particularly during the riots, he had been a beacon of strength for many. Hearing these words from him meant that somebody familiar with the world of black education was responding in an understanding way to what we had to offer.

Hearing the response from the community leader and educator of Alexandra and the affirmation of his colleagues, we knew that our initiative to start with an educational social project was relevant in Alexandra. We, too, "saw the light" at that moment.

CHAPTER V

THE NURSERY SCHOOL INITIATIVE
IN ALEXANDRA TOWNSHIP

Preparing for the Inkanyezi Children's Garden

Pedagogy is love for man,
resulting from knowledge of man.

Rudolf Steiner

Before any plans to start a school initiative in Alexandra could be realized, we had to consult with members of the Alexandra community. Many meetings were held with a steering committee that consisted of people from all shades of the political spectrum in Alexandra. Finally, after months, we were given their blessing. At that, the steering committee dissolved, but not before recommending to us five people who might have an interest in being trained.

Ben, at that time a codirector of the Thusong Youth Centre, who would soon become a parent of the Children's Garden, chose the name *Inkanyezi* for us, the Zulu word for star. He gave the reason that when night sets in and the stars come out one by one, magic descends upon the township. The children love to come out at that time and play outside in the magic of the night.

So, in December 1986, began the training of five people with the intent to choose two as teachers at the nursery school in Alexandra. The first week we had only three people. There was Emily, who twice had worked as a domestic in David's household, initially while his first wife, Betty, was still alive and the second time after Betty had died (more about Emily in chapter 13). There were also Fundie, and Catherine. What they heard in that first week about the incarnation and spiritual origin of the human being immediately struck a deep chord with them, so much so, that Emily insisted the whole story be repeated for the two new people

Elizabeth and Palesa, who joined a bit later.

Thus, once more, in different words, Carol went deeply into the mystery of birth and the wonder of the developing human being and how in the first three years the child deeply experiences all the influences of the people and the environment and how this forms the basis of its future development. She also spoke of the invisible wisdom and will within the child that enables it to learn to walk, to speak, and to think.

If we had not repeated the whole story, Emily said, they could not have become a cohesive group. It was this knowledge about the spiritual reality of the child that would bind them together.

For the next six months we conducted intensive training sessions with these five people. It soon became apparent that it was impossible to choose between any one of them. All had different and valuable qualities with regard to the task at hand. None of them had any formal training except Catherine. The only prerequisite for attending the training course was to have a genuine love for children.

It was an exciting adventure for all of us. Becoming engaged in so many artistic activities was a totally new experience for the trainees and greatly boosted their self-confidence. They found everything equally rewarding: doing speech with Maxine, eurythmy and circle games with Truus, painting and drawing with Claartje, and shadow play and drama with Carol. They also learned to make dolls with Brigitte, who had joined the teacher trainers' group. They even made little baskets out of mealie (corn) leaves.

Steve Burger, the administrator of Alexandra, was so fascinated by these baskets that he kept one with a doll (made by the doll makers described in chapter 6) in it in his office to show any visitor who might be interested how clever hands could make something out of practically nothing.

This training took place at the Baobab Centre in Randburg where we had moved in October 1986. A large donation from Holland for transportation of the trainees made it possible for them to come to our center.

For the last month prior to opening the nursery school in Alexandra, the teachers were able to spend time at the Waldorf School in Bryanston near Johannesburg and observe the nursery school classes there. It was a revelation to them seeing in practice in that school all they had heard during the last months. In addition they were greatly encouraged because the children at the Bryanston nursery school immediately took to them. Thus, after this last month the teachers were keener than ever before to get started on their own. Also it became urgent for them to start earning salaries now that their six months' training was completed.

Finding Housing for the Inkanyezi Children's Garden

While the teachers were in training and the months went by, we realized that it would take longer than expected to start the nursery school on premises to be built for it. With the parents pressing us to begin and also the teachers' need to get started, we found temporary housing in the church building of the Mahon Mission. Rev. Matthew Malele and his colleagues were very enthusiastic and extremely cooperative. They were happy with the idea of being able to contribute something needed and worthwhile to the Alexandra community.

As it turned out, the Mahon Mission Church itself also greatly benefited from its generosity. Because of the fact that the church was going to be upgraded and used so intensively, the building was saved from demolition.

However, we still had to find people who would be willing to build a kitchen for us. Since nursery schools in townships operate from 7:00 a.m. to 4:00 p.m. to accommodate both parents' working, it is necessary to provide two meals a day for the children. Thanks to Stan Goldstein's help, a kitchen was built for us attached to the church. A company in Wynberg helped by paying for the fence around the place.

Young people from the Thusong Youth Centre in Alexandra spent three weeks of their holidays making little wooden chairs and tables for the school with the help of Gavin, one of our friends. It was a time of intensive preparation readying the old church building for receiving the children. We wanted to make it very beautiful for them, a place, where they could feel completely at home.

The Opening of Inkanyezi Children's Garden

In July 1987, we opened the gates for the children and two weeks later celebrated the official opening of the school. Present at this occasion was Pauline, who had married David in whose household Emily had worked. Pauline wrote a letter for those who could not be present at the festive opening of Inkanyezi Children's Garden.

July 18 was a dry and dusty winter day. Of the first visitors who tentatively and cautiously arrived, some had never visited a township before. The cheeky wind blew the smoke from the squatters' fires into the faces of the people seated on the church benches, arranged for the occasion in a large circle outside.

It was a mixed array of people sitting there together. Standing right outside the fence were the people living in the shacks around the church, who also wanted to be part of this special event in the township.

Ben Mhlongo, chairman of our steering committee, welcomed the guests and told how having his daughter in the Children's Garden already had changed his family's routine; before each meal they now hold hands to say a blessing.

After many more speeches we enjoyed the spirited dancing of the young gumboot dancers. We had met most of them before when they spent a week with us for an arts and crafts program. Now they had a special gift of their own to offer us.

We originally admitted 30 children as planned. But then on a daily basis we had to comfort parents standing at the gate with a child on one hand and money for the school fees in the other, hoping to gain admission to the school. At times it was very hard to have to refuse them, but, with 37 children we felt the limit had been reached.

The teacher trainers suggested a stipend program for those parents who were unable to pay, but the people of Alexandra said "everybody must pay the same." We tried to keep the fees very low, in fact so low that they only paid for the two meals a day. The remaining expenditures, especially the teachers' salaries had to come from our fund-raising efforts.

The Children

Very soon the 37 children settled down and became a group that really belonged together. Most children fitted in easily but some gave us cause for concern. It was to be expcted that some children would emerge from township life with scars in their souls. We had two children whose aggressiveness constantly brought the others to tears. Yet, they were so sensitive themselves that when the recorder was played, they put their hands over their ears to block out the sound because it was too harsh for them.

We experienced another difficulty with children who came from the rural areas. There they were being brought up by their grandparents and other relatives. Now that places were available in a nursery school, the parents brought them back again to Alexandra. They were very shy, much more introverted and insecure. For those children it was not at all easy to integrate with the much more sophisticated children who had been raised in the township.

At first some children were overwhelmed, having crept out of a little squatter hut to face this big space with beautiful wooden furniture and an abundance of things to play with. As the weeks went by, they became more comfortable with the new situation, little people in their own right, confident enough to greet us when we came to the school.

It was amazing to see how soon the children were happily engaged in their watercolor painting. Claartje would let a doll show them how to paint. The children would then copy what the doll had shown them. This was one way of getting around the language problem, as the children knew hardly any English. We teacher trainers knew some Zulu words but not enough to converse with the children. Yet, the children often would come excitedly trying to tell us the latest news.

At one time I asked the teacher what they had been trying to tell me. I was rather disappointed when I heard that they had been asking if I could bring them toy guns to school next time. When the children play outside, they often pretend to have guns and shoot at each other. This is understandable, as they daily see soldiers with guns. Also, many of them have been exposed to a lot of violence, rioting, and shooting, either in reality or on TV. Obviously, we will have to find creative ways of diverting them into playing different kinds of games.

With regard to discipline, the teachers were facing a major challenge. In South Africa it is quite usual to punish children harshly. Many teachers hold the ruler in their hands as a constant reminder that physical punishment is close at hand. That way children live in constant fear of the adults and cannot unfold freely. Our teachers also had grown up under this harsh regimentation. In the Waldorf School in Bryanston they saw that children could behave well without any heavy discipline. But how would we change this where children were used to very strict discipline?

It was clear this situation called for ingenuity in having a disciplined classroom atmosphere without hurting the tender souls of the young children. The teachers knew that to grow up with confidence and creativity, fear had to be minimized as much as possible. Months later the teachers proved how well they succeeded. The teachers and children communicate very well without any harsh words having to be said.

Another thing the children were not used to was to be in a world completely geared to their needs. Black children seldom have any toys. Life is a very serious business for them. Much is expected of them in terms of work from an early age. It is not unusual to see a four- or five-year-old child with a little baby brother or sister strapped to its back.

The children also were not used to play. We had to sit on the floor with them and show them how to build with the wooden blocks or play with the dolls. This was important because play is the major avenue of learning through which the child reaches his surrounding world and learns about himself.

As Mary Sibiya, a high school science teacher taking on the training of preschool teachers said:

> Through play the child must be reached in its totality and be helped to develop not only the skills for learning and living, but also attitudes and values essential to the attainment of worthwhile goals in life. Alternative education therefore should focus on play as the best way of preparing the preschool child for the future.

Another observation was that most people in the township lost the feeling of being connected with nature. In our teacher training courses we make a point of, for example, building nature tables with the teachers. Subsequently they tell us that after that their eyes begin to open for the wonders of nature and they begin to see the different forms of trees, leaves, and clouds. Their souls needed to be awakened to the rich gifts of nature even in surroundings where nature is not cultivated and where there are a lot of things one would rather not see at all. Being able to see the beauty of a rainbow, the teachers become able to awaken wonder in the souls of the children for this open book of nature there for those who learned to perceive with their hearts as well as with their senses.

Festival celebrations also created special experiences for the children. On the last day of school before the Christmas holidays, we have a pre-Christmas celebration with all the parents and children. In the first year, the teachers and teacher trainers performed a Christmas play that related to the situation in the township. It was well received by a big audience. When the rain finally started to beat on the corrugated iron roof of the church and the words could no longer be understood, big and small started to sing and dance together. It was a joyful ending of the Christmas festival and of the work with the children in 1987.

What Happened After the First Year?

Our waiting list for openings at the Inkanyezi Children's Garden grew longer. We were given a pre-fab building and were able to have it erected on the church grounds. Thus we could admit 30 additional children.

After the five teachers had their training for the nursery school, we decided that not only two but all five should stay and take four classes instead of two as originally planned. It was an important decision with far-reaching consequences in the years to come. With only 600 children out of 15,000 having places in nursery schools, one cannot easily make small decisions to serve only a few children. The needs are too overwhelming.

Thus we knew we had to build at least four classrooms for 30 children each. It was the task of the Teachers College in conjunction with the teacher trainers, the Finance Committee, and the Parents Committee to work toward the goal of raising the necessary funds for a combined nursery school/workshop complex.

S.M. Goldstein already had donated the architectural plans as a gift for our project. Everyone was pleased with them, the teachers most of all, who wanted the buildings to be similar to the Bryanston Waldorf Nursery School. It certainly was going to be an unusual structure in the township: buildings arranged in a big curve with a covered corridor with beautifully shaped arches all along the outside. And, of course, we were going to paint it in a special way, using pastel colors inside and outside to make it even more lively and a real expression of what we mean by a Children's Garden. In the end it turned out quite differently, as will be told, but the force of our imagination of what could be carried us a long way.

Meanwhile, our young children were growing older. Many parents already approached us requesting that we continue to work in the same way with the children throughout their school years. We were fortunate that we did not have to face this decision immediately since our children were still too young to go to primary school. But, in 1988, we had to prepare for the beginning of a primary school on Waldorf educational principles. This also meant having to get more intensively involved with the training of primary school teachers not only at the Funda Centre in Soweto but also in Alexandra itself.

48

CHAPTER VI

ORGANIZING WORKSHOPS IN ALEXANDRA TOWNSHIP

The First Workshop in Alexandra

When we began peparing for the Inkanyezi Children's Garden in 1986, we saw an opportunity to teach a few local residents some badly needed skills and in doing so create things that were needed for the Children's Garden. It was our hope that this would be the beginning of workshop activities around the school. As it later proved, this was easier envisioned than done. However, the first workshop came off splendidly.

It was the wood workshop where the wooden furniture for the nursery school was made. Gavin was available as a woodwork instructor. The power tools were donated by Black & Decker. Guy arranged for the donation of the wood and additional tools needed and 12 youngsters from Alexandra were prepared to give three weeks of their Christmas holidays to help make the furniture.

It turned out to be a great success. The atmosphere was splendid. Although the young people had not worked with power tools before, they handled them easily. We promised to feed them but had not quite counted on their large appetites. In the end, 50 chairs and 20 tables were produced. One of the young men asked if he could do a project of his own and so he made himself a well-functioning and beautiful easel.

The young people came away with new skills and much confidence in their own abilities and creativity. Every time people see the chairs and tables they comment on how beautiful they are. They cost more than plastic furniture, but they are friendly to the eye. The grain of the wood is interesting to look at and when one touches it, one can feel that there is something alive. We wanted the children to be in touch with real things from nature because they are much more alive than things made out of man-made materials and therefore also make the children more alive.

We were allowed to conduct the woodworking workshop at Entokozweni Child Welfare Centre. It meant taking all the tools home every evening. It also meant having to deal with many electrical black-outs and power failures. Two weeks during that Christmastime some organizations forced people not to use any electrical lights but sit with a candle and remember all the people who gave their lives in the struggle or were still in detention.

At the same time a boycott was enforced on the people of the township to avoid buying anything in a shop owned by whites. Also, people were not allowed to leave the township to go to work. At those times it is better for white people not to be seen in the township. Such is life in the township, filled with obstacles and difficulties. On the other hand, many good things are also constantly happening.

The Inkanyezi Rainbow Project: Making Dolls

In 1986, while we were preparing for the Inkanyezi Children's Garden, Alexandra had an unemployment rate of 45%. We wanted to contribute something meaningful to that problem by providing work, as little as it might be. First of all, this meant teaching skills. We could see that many factors had to fall into place at the same time, not the least being having the right instructors who recognized the social healing aspect as more important than even teaching the actual skills.

We knew we needed soft toys for the children. Rather than obtaining these dolls from elsewhere, would it be possible to involve some people from the Alexandra community by having them make such soft toys, specifically dolls? The big question was: whom could we interest in making the specific dolls we wanted?

From what we knew about the township, we were aware that good things also happen there. For instance, it was amazing to see what was done by the community for the old people. There were several luncheon clubs where old people could come to meet each other and where a meal was prepared for them. People who still were able to walk could go to different places for a free meal during the week. Also, big Christmas celebrations were organized for them each year with food parcels for everybody to take home. Once a year there might have been an outing to the seaside. There was also a large party for four residents of Alexandra who had reached the honorable ages of over 95.

It so happened that while we were working on readying the Inkanyezi Children's Garden, we met with such a group of old women at the weekly luncheon club in Entokozweni. We spoke with them—through a translator, of course—and asked them if they would like the idea of making soft cloth dolls for the Children's Garden. We were amazed at their immediate enthusiastic response. So, Sue McCabe started to work with them.

The immediate big problem was where to set up the workshop. Earlier in the year, the Alexandra Town Council had offered us a big space next to the beer hall. There were many unemployed people around there. They were lining all the walls of the beer hall, sitting on crates and tins or just on the floor. Our Steering Committee for the Children's Garden decided immediately that that space would not be suitable. The beer hall was located very close to the police station and the Town Council. Young people would not want to show themselves in that area. We had to take their advice even though we knew it would be very difficult to find another place in Alexandra.

A possibility then opened up to use the kitchen of Itlhokomeleng Old Age Home for the doll-making workshop. This meant a great sacrifice by both the cooks and the doll-makers, as the cooks would have to do the cooking right around the chairs of the doll-makers and the doll-makers would have to sit and work in a steaming kitchen in the hot African summer. Nevertheless, some of the middle-aged ladies from the Entokozweni luncheon club who still could walk well came with Sue every morning to make dolls. The group grew steadily in size and so did their skills at making dolls.

How the Dollmaking Continued

There were ups and downs, but on the whole, the doll workshop became a real success. A setback occurred—at least for the workshop—when Sue decided to go to England for additional training in speech and drama.

Losing Sue was felt as a great loss by the ladies, as a wonderful group spirit had developed with Sue. While the ladies were happy to receive money for their work, the peaceful, co-operative way they worked together was even more important to them. But soon Elsa declared herself ready to step in and take her place. Although the ladies knew the whole procedure very well, someone needed to be there to help and guide them and see that the quality of the dolls produced was up to standard.

In the meantime, the women decided that they were a self-help group and personally could be responsible for the quality and standard of the dolls made. They only needed some help from the outside to get materials and take the finished dolls to different nursery schools and childminders. We were glad to see this real progress and development of self-confidence and pride in their work.

Since we began almost six years ago, the doll workshop has made steady progress. Of the original group, one or two people are still with us. Most of the 20 women now working with the project are young women from rural areas. Usually, such women leave their children at home with relatives and go to Johannesburg to see if they can earn some money. As the unemployment rate in Alexandra in 1993 climbed to 55%, it was extremely difficult for them to find work and even more difficult to survive by selling vegetables or *mealies* (Afrikaans word for maize) at the roadside. It

was heartrending, therefore, to hear what the women had to say at our Christmas festival when everyone spoke of what it meant for them to be involved with the Inkanyezi project. Many had lost all hope of even surviving, not to speak of sending any money to their families. Now they had new hope for the future. It gave them security to be part of this self-help project.

The doll makers are from different nations: Venda, Zulu, Sotho, Xhosa, Pedi, and Shangaan. They represent the new South Africa in that, besides black people, there is Rose, for a few years already the responsible and most appreciated supervisor, who is colored and myself, who am white.

According to the language they speak, about one third of all black people in South Africa belong to the Sotho group, whereas the Zulus, Xhosas, Pondas, and Swazis belong to the Nguni group, whose languages, though different from each other, share a similar structural uniformity.

Quite different again are the Vendas of Venda, the independent homeland in the northernmost part of South Africa, with about 400,000 inhabitants. The Shangaan/Tsonga people, numbering about 800,000 live mainly in Gazankulu which is also located in northern Transvaal. The languages of the Shangaan and Vendas as well as their customs and traditions, are different again from those of the Sotho and the Nguni peoples.

It is not easy to truly fathom the complexity of life in South Africa and then one has not even added the Afrikaans and English speaking peoples. There are bilingual countries such as Belgium, for example, which have struggled for centuries with the problem of how to keep their identity and how to deal with the fear of being dominated by people from another language group. When one experiences how the women of our doll maker's group, representing a variety of languages and cultures, cope and communicate with each other, one can only be filled with admiration for their flexibility and willingness to surmount the language problem.

Since 1989, the doll makers' workshop is located on the property of the Inkanyezi Waldorf Centre. This provides the doll makers with the opportunity of placing their own children in the nursery school at an early age. The school, children and teachers, in turn, have an opportunity to see people making beautiful things with their own hands.

In addition, the income of each doll maker is now three times the amount it used to be. At Christmas, each woman receives an extra bonus. They also get weekly donations of vegetables and other foodstuffs which are given to the project. Thus our hope of being able to help in a social way in the bleak township of Alexandra has been fruitful via this avenue.

Another doll making group just started in Soweto in connection with the Sikhulise Waldorf School. The initiative in Madietane would also like to start a doll making group.

What Is Special About These Dolls?

In speaking about the dolls and the process of making them, we need to mention what kind of dolls they are. The type of doll we wanted to make had been developed over the years by teachers working in the international Waldorf schools. Dolls manufactured by machines often have distorted faces and bodies, and most are so detailed they leave nothing to the imagination. The Waldorf doll, on the other hand, wants to let children experience more truthfully the basic image of the human being. Like the human being, the dolls are not perfect but from experience we have learned that they greatly appeal to the imagination of the child.

Also, because it is part of our philosophy that young children should touch and be in touch with nature, we are very strict in using only pure natural materials for these dolls, such as cotton, wool, and silk. This added another obstacle to making the dolls in South Africa, as finding pure natural materials there was very difficult since most of the available fibers are man-made.

Of course, other groups also make dolls—quite different from ours, though. In addition, they go about the production process in a different way: by having each woman handle only one aspect of the doll making process. Some people will sew, some stuff, some will make the faces or whatever else has to be done. We, on the other hand, believe it is most important that in making dolls resembling the true image of the human being each woman starts and completes her own doll. It is quite different to complete the whole process yourself than work on an assembly line. It is a wholesome experience for one woman to make and finish a doll. We experienced that the women put so much love into making the doll that it sometimes was difficult for them to part with it. They also think of the child that will be playing with their particular doll. On the name tag attached to each doll's wrist, the name of the person who made the doll is written. Thus, the personal element is being maintained.

Over the years, the doll makers' skills have steadily increased. In the most recent years they were at the point of not only making dolls relating to their own tribe or "nation" as they call it, but any kind of doll that is needed at a certain moment. They can do this because they are remarkably creative and resourceful.

Marketing the Dolls

It turned out that people liked the dolls. We started calling them the Waldorf dolls. White people wanted to buy them. Unfortunately, soon after we started the doll making, there was a break-in, and all the dolls we were going to sell were stolen. From that moment onward, Sue would take all dolls and materials home every evening.

A good friend offered to sell the dolls together with her own pottery ware at the Organic Village Market, the fund-raising project for the Bryanston Waldorf School. There, twice a week, the dolls can be purchased.

Then, a very good thing happened in that AECI (a South African industrial firm that produces explosives) heard about our work and decided to give us a grant so that we could provide the other nursery schools in Alexandra with dolls. Until now, mainly white people had bought the dolls. Now, we were finally able to also provide black children with these beautiful dolls.

There was a problem, however, in that black children hardly have any toys and therefore do not know how to play with them, as mentioned before. In white nursery schools little strollers or prams are available for the children's dolls, maybe even a dollhouse. Not so, of course, in our little school where we provide the children with carrying cloths. That way, in play, they can carry the babies tied to their backs as their mothers and older siblings do.

First we had to make sure the nursery school teachers started to get a feeling for the fact that a doll is not the same as any other toy that one can put away on a shelf or a cupboard. A doll is like a child, so children must be able to care for the doll as if it were their child. The baby doll must stay around and can't be locked away. In short, there is a whole culture around dolls. Black children don't have this. Without such a culture it was no good giving the dolls away to nursery schools. The idea of playing with dolls needed to be introduced to the teachers first.

Selling dolls in the market place calls for different qualities than those required for making dolls. As black people in South Africa are not at all used to buying toys for their children, we could not hope to find customers in Alexandra. However, many dolls have been bought by employers for the children of their employees, and that is wonderful. It is, however, still the tourist market that is most rewarding financially.

In addition, many Waldorf schools all over the world have been successfully selling our dolls at their St. Martin's or Christmas bazaars. If I am overseas on a fund-raising trip, the dolls sell like hot cakes. Thus I do no longer have to worry about whether or not there is enough money at the end of the month to pay the women for their work. Yet, with more women wanting and able to make the dolls, we have to secure additional orders.

From letters we received from customers, we were happy to see that the dolls became like little ambassadors speaking about Africa and spreading good will.

Teaching More Skills and Making More Things

In the early days of doll making we were fortunate to have Brigitte with us. She had been a handicrafts teacher for many years in different Waldorf schools in Germany and after that she taught crafts in Africa for 3 years, often bringing African crafts back to the black people. In addition to teaching our nursery school teachers how to make dolls, she taught them to make little baskets from *mealie* leaves, as mentioned earlier. This is done hardly anywhere in South Africa. All *mealie* leaves are thrown away as useless. Here, however, people were shown what one can do with discarded materials.

Brigitte had many other skills, one of which was working with leather. She was prepared to get started with a group of unemployed people to teach them leather crafts with the idea that in the end some people might become self-employed. Once again, Marjorie Manganye, who had started Itlhokomeleng Old Age Home gave us space to use her storeroom for this workshop. It was a sad thing that out of eight people only Rachel Twala continued until, three months later, Brigitte had to go back to Germany.

Amazingly, after working for some months on her own, Rachel found some people who wanted to learn the skills from her. We were able to give her a good boost by providing her with some bags of sheepskin cutoffs as well as some tools for working with leather. In 1988 a group of six people were producing many pairs of slippers a day. It was Rachel's good fortune that autumn and winter were approaching when people needed warm slippers. It might even be possible to sell the slippers to a big shoe outlet in Wynberg, just around the corner.

The most amazing thing was that Rachel, who had been out of work for many years and had been very depressed, became a confident and hard-working entrepreneur.

Aside from the women mentioned, there are now also the students at Baobab, who not only need an income for payment of tuition, living expenses, and transportation, but also have to learn to be entrepreneurs. Future nursery school teachers need business and bookkeeping skills in addition to pedagogical skills. Future Waldorf teachers need an understanding of financial details, because they will have to concern themselves not only with pedagogical but also with administrative matters. It is important that a variety of income generating projects will be initiated where these students can find partial employment.

In addition we now have a group of four parents—formerly unemployed—who have started to manufacture indoor slippers, also called eurythmy shoes. I knew there would be an international market for them if we made them attractive enough. Now they can be ordered in bright African colors. It is heartwarming to see the positive change in a person who has been unemployed for a long time. It is our task and wish to create more opportunities for work, at first for parents of our schoolchildren and Baobab students and also for others. There is no limit to what can and should be done.

We are negotiating about a big factory on the other side of the street from the Inkanyezi Waldorf Centre or we may be able to use the Alexandra People's Market for small manufacturing units. These plans are still on the drawing board. However, with the help of many supporters in the industrial world and with development aid from foreign countries, we hope these intentions, like others before, will become reality.

CHAPTER VII

THE PRIMARY SCHOOL INITIATIVE IN ALEXANDRA TOWNSHIP

How the Inkanyezi Waldorf Centre Began

It was through the determination of parents of the first group of nursery school children that the school came into existence. They soon saw positive development in their children and were determined that ways would be found for them to continue with this kind of education.

It was then, in March 1988, that Theo crossed our path again. We had met him some years ago, after he returned from Emerson College in England, where he attended a two-year Waldorf Teacher Training course. This kind of education very much appealed to him. Having had a good education in a private school himself, he was adamant about giving black children a chance to have a quality education.

When we first met Theo we had not yet started with our work in the townships, and Theo felt it was important for him to get a teacher's degree from a university. So he left for Cape Town and obtained a teacher's degree. Degree in hand, he returned to Johannesburg, just at the right time.

In December 1988, a meeting took place at the Mahon Mission Church with those parents who wanted to continue Waldorf education for their children. We also invited Theo, who so spoke to the hearts of the parents they immediately asked him to become their children's teacher. One parent offered his garage, and though the space was very small even for eight children—the number Theo started with—it was a paradise.

In the presence of the children, Claartje made a big wall painting of the story of the Three Kings and soon the walls were decorated with all the paintings and drawings the children themselves so eagerly made. It really was a special pioneering

situation, the beginnings of an independent school in Alexandra, using a totally different approach to education than any people had experienced.

As the garage had only one small window, the rolltop door stayed open most of the time. The garage was directly at the roadside, which had its positive as well as its negative aspects. The negative aspect was to have to listen for hours to the loudly blaring pop music coming from the car of the ice-cream vendor on the other side of the road. The positive aspect was that when people walked past and wondered what was going on, they would bend down to look underneath the rolltop door, and next morning they would come to enroll their children. It did not take long, therefore, until there were 16 children. Now, the garage was really full and we urgently had to find an alternate solution. The lessons in artistic movement (eurythmy) were especially difficult to give for sheer lack of space.

How the Inkanyezi Waldorf Centre Grew

As so many times in crisis situations, we received an unexpected phone call from a business woman in South Africa who had heard about our work, was convinced that Waldorf education should become much more accessible on a grassroots level for a broad spectrum of people, and offered us money to build a school. That required much planning and also more money than she had offered, but at least we suddenly had the means for a better solution, albeit again only a temporary one.

Some time earlier, we had been able to acquire a piece of land from the Town Council. That actually was a miracle, as land is extremely scarce in Alexandra. When we went to the Town Council again at a later date and presented our whole vision for the school, including a nursery, a primary school, and a high school, we were given a second plot adjacent to the one already allotted to us.

Suddenly, we had to scramble, as scores of squatters (later called "homeless people"), lured by promises of work, came to Alexandra by the truckload. On the truck with them came poles and corrugated sheets for walls and roofs of shacks to live in, and they started occupying every empty lot they could find. Just before they took possession of our land, we were able to fence it in. What a sigh of relief, because it would have been next to impossible to remove them once they occupied the land.

Our property was actually surrounded in back and on the sides by people living in such shacks made of corrugated sheets. They were dwellings of no more than three-by-three meters without any sanitary facilities and no electricity but with garbage heaps growing by the day. Not until much later, at the end of a long spell of terrible violence and unrest and after the shooting of seven people, did these squatters move their shacks to another location away from the camp of their political enemies.

With the garage becoming too small and a new class expected, we had to look for an interim solution until a real school building could be constructed. An 18-meters long prefabricated hut was obtained and erected on the property by January 1990, just in time to accommodate the new class. The number of children in Theo's class increased drastically and the new class teacher, Lorna, immediately admitted 40 children.

We were just as lucky to find Lorna. Like Theo, Lorna had already been studying the works of Rudolf Steiner in order to understand the background of Waldorf education. She was studying education at a university in Cape Town, when we

approached her. Rather than continuing to learn teaching methods that did not appeal to her, she preferred to have her training directly at the two existing Waldorf schools in Cape Town. Thanks to the help and cooperation of the teachers in both schools, Lorna was able to gain an overall experience of Waldorf education in action.

Lorna had to prepare herself for a demanding task. As was the case with Theo, Lorna and her children at first had no common language. Both Theo's and Lorna's mother tongue is Afrikaans. The children, on the other hand, came from different African language groups such as Zulu, Sotho, Xhosa, and Afrikaans.

It is always quite amazing how black children manage to communicate with each other, considering the variety of language backgrounds. But now, upon entering school, our children's mutual language had to be English. Luckily, the parents are very much in favor of their children learning English as early as possible. Thus far, each new first class took about three months to become fairly fluent in English.

In 1991, another class was added, and Wiebke became the class teacher. She had years of teaching experience at the Michael Mount Waldorf School in Johannesburg and in a black school.

In 1992 Mosidi joined us. She had received her Waldorf teacher training at Novalis College in Cape Town thanks to sponsorship by the Australian Embassy. With her arrival the teachers' college became truly integrated into colored, white, and black.

At the beginning of 1993, the Inkanyezi Waldorf Centre had five classes with 190 children, as well as 75 children in three nursery school classes. Overall, a total of eight nursery schools had been started in different townships and rural areas by people inspired by the Waldorf ideas we shared through the Baobab courses.

In many ways, a township school is quite different from other schools. The teachers in our school are also mother and father figures for the children. Because of the appalling hygienic conditions, children often come with sores and other ailments. Luckily, the school's medicine cupboard, combined with Theo's knowledge of the different *mutis* (Zulu word for medicine), brings relief in each instance.

A number of children are on full or partial tuition. Even though R 100.00 (approximately U.S. $33.00) a month, for an independent school receiving no state subsidy, is an extremely small fee, for many parents it is a substantial amount to pay. Very often, the whole extended family—uncles, aunts, grandparents—all pool their resources to get the fees together. But if there are no family members to help, and parents have only some "piece work" now and then, it is a blessing that we can offer at least a partial financial relief.

For this reason, it is quite wonderful that children from Waldorf schools overseas have taken it upon themselves to sponsor children at our school. A whole class makes a commitment for one scholarship. One school in Germany is sponsoring 17 children in such a way! A class in Switzerland is sponsoring three children.

We are not keeping all the grants for the Inkanyezi school alone, because our sister schools in other townships (described in following chapters), are also greatly in need of grants. A change has taken place in the way we look at the whole scholarship program. After lengthy discussions, we came to the conclusion that it would be better to deviate from the individual link-up between "godparents" and "godchildren" and instead have people choose one of the school initiatives, making monthly payments

either to a children's fund or to a teacher's fund. That was our idea. However, in reality, people felt more confident if the money they were giving was used directly for the education of a specific child.

We have often been asked why we actually started a school in a township proper, as most independent multiracial schools are situated in white residential areas. This question would surface especially during those times when we had to close Inkanyezi because of unrest. At one point, we brought this issue to a full parents' meeting, because we were eager to know what they thought of it. The response was overwhelmingly in favor of having the school in Alexandra itself. The parents found that the Inkanyezi school represented the new era and was seen as a beacon of hope. For so long, people had been forced to live in separate areas. A normalization of life would only come about if good things, such as the Inkanyezi school, could happen in the township and form a link to the African way of life.

The people visiting our school call it an oasis amidst the surrounding devastation. Yet, there has been a considerable loss of enrollment as parents were afraid for their children. With the decrease in enrollment, a really difficult financial situation ensued. More than ever before we need outside help to carry the school through this difficult period.

Philosophy of Waldorf Education Implemented at Inkanyezi

From the very beginning, we were sure of one thing, namely, that the Inkanyezi school should not be an elite school but open for all children who would find their way to us. Having a school right in the township is a way of saying yes to people's lives in the township. Taking children into the white areas means that they have to adapt fully to the Western ways of education. The parents are very keen for their children to learn proper English from an early age, yet, they are also happy that their children are exposed to the African myths, stories, and traditions.

The Waldorf way of educating requires a completely different approach. It is much closer to the imaginative world of folk tales and mythologies. Through all the grades of primary school, the children are exposed to the main mythologies of prominent cultural epochs, from the folk tales originating in the part of the world in which the child lives to the legends of saints and traditional fables to the mythologies of the ancient Indians,

Persians, Egyptians, Greeks, and other cultures. Also, the child is really engaged in his feeling and willing by having all subjects steeped in art, in painting, drawing, clay modeling, music, drama, and artistic movement.

The children are also actively engaged in games and movement activities. Eurythmy accompanies them from kindergarten through high school. The children learn to play the recorder in class I. Learning is so enjoyable, that they never want to miss a day. The parents really have problems during the holidays, as the children want nothing more than to be back in school.

When potential donors visit the school, they are amazed by the relationship between the teachers and the children. The children accept the teacher as the authority, but not because the teacher behaves in an authoritarian way. Visitors also experience how a class can continue working quietly for quite a while, even if the teacher has to see to some urgent matter outside the classroom.

What really holds a school together? What is the inspiration, not only for each individual teacher, but for the whole body of teachers? It is the shared conviction that each child has a spiritual aspect that needs guidance in the ways of the world but also brings new impulses from the spiritual world. Unless the teacher makes room for these realities and allows for individual talents and capacities to unfold, they will be lost.

The College of Teachers has the task of keeping this impulse alive in each teacher, by always creating time for the study of the developing human being and by renewing—together and alone— the deep commitment to the work. Teaching must be experienced as a vocation, a calling. Every morning before school starts, all teachers come together to contemplate their task and to call on the help of the spiritual world for their work with the children. It is the free choice of each teacher to be part of that meeting or not. However, the teachers who do take part, always feel how their day is carried by this common activity.

As the Inkanyezi school is in an exceptional situation by being one of the very few independent schools situated in a township, it needs a lot of protection. It is unthinkable that one would rely on the usual ways of protection like high walls or alarm systems. Of course, there is a high fence and we have burglar bars, which speak a language. But the most real protection comes from having a children's service once a week. After the procedures and content had been explained to the parents, and they had been invited to attend one of those services, they were all pleased to let their children take part. By children and adults alike, this weekly service is experienced as the core of the work. The children show this by being extremely attentive and quiet. A special part of the service is that each child is individually addressed and that he or she, in turn, responds individually.

Why We Called the Inkanyezi Primary School "Inkanyezi Centre"

From the start, we all felt that the word *school* carried a burden of limited connotations. Already, when we began the nursery school or preschool, as it is mostly called, we felt quite uncomfortable with that word, especially when used for young children. With the name "Inkanyezi Children's Garden," we wanted to express a friendlier and more comprehensive approach to learning. Of course, the word kindergarten—taken from the German—has become an accepted name worldwide for a place where young children can be involved in the adventure of exploring the world around them. We translated kindergarten, meaning a garden for children, into children's garden.

When the time came for finding the right name for the Inkanyezi primary school, we were aware of many young people and adults who would have loved to have had a Waldorf education and whose lives we would like to have the opportunity to enrich. That is why we called our school a centre. For us, the word centre indicates the relationship between the school and the community and is, therefore, not meant to be an island unto itself. We would like the community of Alexandra to be part of the impulse that is living at Inkanyezi. A variety of activities should be launched, depending primarily on the human and financial resources available. We contemplate courses in life skills, social skills, parenting, different arts and crafts, and practical-technical skills.

The question of how to finance those plans is a very real one, indeed. The business community often has the leading edge in knowing the direction in which certain developments should go. There is a definite awareness of the fact that the townships must be urgently developed in all areas. If such development does not take place, they will increasingly become festering sores and breeding grounds of crime.

Already, the Inkanyezi Centre is seen as a beacon of hope. It can have a new reality for the whole community of Alexandra. It can also have positive consequences for the surrounding industrial areas as well as for Sandton, a very wealthy district. According to the Sandton Chamber of Commerce, Sandton is the most affluent district of Johannesburg, home of influential decision-makers. Though Alexandra and Sandton are in such close proximity, they are worlds apart.

Looking Toward the Future

Once a year, all the teachers make an effort to create in their minds a picture of the school for the years to come. We may close our eyes and just wait for an image of what may happen in the future. It is remarkable, how similar the descriptions of the pictures are that people then share with each other.

Our school situation can be compared to a seed. It is still very young, full of promise, but not yet completely formed. We hope that one day, it will grow into a beautiful plant. Even if we can already anticipate the direction in which the school is going, we do realize that the development of the school largely depends on the commitment of all those who comprise the school community: the children, the parents, the teachers, and, to a certain extent, the donors. In the same way the seed depends on the right conditions of soil, weather, and care by human beings, so the harmonious growth of the school depends on the positive input and healthy communication between all involved.

It has been obvious to the parents that once the children were exposed to Waldorf education, they should continue with it. This was the case when the first threshold had to be crossed from nursery to primary school. A much bigger threshold will be the one from primary to high school.

In our vision, the Inkanyezi children will be with us until the time comes they are ready to go to work or into more specialized training situations, colleges or universities. We want to be so versatile in our approach that there will be a variety of choices for our young pupils in terms of going either into a practical or more academic direction. Of course, the ideal is to combine both. It should be clear that a matric examination, allowing them to go on to university studies, is not the ultimate door to success in life. The young people graduating from our school—or from other Waldorf schools for that matter—should have developed a high degree of creativity, ingenuity, social skills, practical and academic intelligence, so that they can make a success of their lives.

Throughout the years in school, we try to direct the children's creative abilities gradually into a conscious and controlled creativity so that they can transform it into a sound attitude toward work. In the first few years, the curriculum leads the children from knitting to crocheting, embroidering, sewing, and knotting. Both boys and girls develop the skillful use of their fingers and hands. Other practical activities include baking bread, gardening, and forestry work. Later on, woodwork, basket weaving, copper work, bookbinding, spinning, and weaving are added. The finished products very likely will instill a sense of pride and security in the children.

Even though primarily basic skills are developed, they combine two important components: a technical-practical one and an artistic one. In the highest grades, the pupils are finally exposed to work with iron. Learning all those crafts directs their need to acquire an identity, at first vaguely felt, into an evermore concrete effort to become independent in their judgments, decision making, and actions. If learning is too abstract, it molds human beings in such a way that they can easily become too far removed from the concrete realities of life.

In Germany, there is a Waldorf school in which high school students can learn a trade (electronics, mechanics, metalwork, dress making, and carpentry), or train to become nursery school teachers. Simultaneously, they can also do matriculation. Those who decide to do both, matric and a vocational training course, are required to stay in school for an additional year.

In due course, the Inkanyezi Waldorf Centre will find out what is right for its specific situation. The educators in South Africa, in consultation with parents, are seeking new ways. Not only in the world of black education is there great dissatisfaction with the way in which schools have been run, but also in white education. Much research has been done about the real purpose of education. Why then are there so many high school dropouts worldwide? What happens if schools are disconnected from the concrete realities of life? Usually, students receive no nourishment for their souls and their emotional growth. They feel imprisoned and not recognized in their true being. They seldom develop genuine respect for their teachers, because they themselves do not experience respect from them. Education is so much more than merely an intellectual exercise. Above all, education has to do with social development.

69

In the effort to find new ways in education, we are becoming acutely aware of the contribution that can be made by Africa, and the exclamation "Africa, we need you!" becomes ever more meaningful. It is the heart that is needed in education!

On the whole, parents want the very best for their children. But which model is the very best, they ask? Is it the type of education we received ourselves? Did it really satisfy us? Do we want to make sure that our children find jobs after leaving school? Of course, we do. The main question is how will our children stand in life and in their chosen field of work? Will they as young adults be able to make an original contribution in their work situation? Will they be capable of becoming leaders in their chosen fields? Can they become role models for those young people who come after them?

Parents will have to occupy themselves increasingly with all these questions in order to overcome the stereotyped way of thinking about university matriculation as the ultimate answer for success in life. The Inkanyezi Waldorf Centre will need many sessions with its parents to discuss these issues in depth. The older generation, including myself, received mostly a stifling education. It was definitely not an "education towards freedom," as Waldorf education attempts to be.

Freedom can be the result of developing higher qualities of soul during the school years. One of the trustees of the Centre for the Art of Living, who himself grew up in Alexandra, one day asked the question:

How can one continue the learning process in life in order to come to those most necessary qualities of imagination, inspiration, and intuition?

Children are the most valuable assets in life. They are the future. We, who must guide the younger generation, must do so in harmony with the spirits of progress and the *Zeitgeist*, the spirit of our time. The past can hardly guide us. We must be open to what the future really asks from all of us.

CHAPTER VIII

CHILDREN AND PARENTS
IN ALEXANDRA TOWNSHIP

The Children

Many children in Alexandra were already quite damaged from having to live in the township environment. We had two children, for instance, who were very aggressive, as small as they were; they knew only scratching, biting, kicking, or anything that would hurt the other, be it child or adult. Our school physician pointed out that the children probably had already been damaged in the womb, because the mothers did not have good nutrition during pregnancy. And yet—to jump a little ahead—five years later, those very same boys are working very hard in school and are quite well socialized.

This example is just one of many showing the impact of the school on the life of the children. Many could easily have become *tsotsis* (Afrikaans slang word denoting youngsters in township gangs) and could have joined the ranks of the countless children and young people who are turning the townships into unsafe and dangerous places.

Inkanyezi Waldorf Centre, the primary school growing out of the Inkanyezi Children's Garden, could easily be a school twice its size because of the overwhelming requests for admission. In the spring of 1992, each class had 45 children. To admit more children into a class would definitely dilute the quality of education they now receive.

With the enormous influx of homeless people into the township, there are more than 90,000 children of school age. Only about 20,000 of them are actually attending schools. In the high schools in Alex—as the township is usually called—individual classes comprise up to 100 pupils, with equipment and materials available for only about 40.

The situation is highly frustrating, not only for the students but also for the teachers. Although the Inkanyezi school is making a contribution, it is only a drop in the ocean of vast needs. At this stage, what is important is not so much the number of children we are able to care for, but to show a new direction in education.

One can be amazed at how parents under these dreadful circumstances are able to keep the life of the family together and install strong values in their children. Of course, this is not always the case. We also have situations where parents or, often, single mothers were totally unable to cope. The children had to fend for themselves and ended up roaming the streets with gangs. Sometimes, parents were so engaged in the political struggle that they were continuously away from home attending meetings across the country. That is what we encountered when an 11-year-old boy broke into the nursery school—at that time still located in the Mahon Mission Church—and vandalized the rooms.

At one time, one of our children, only nine years old, threatened other children with a knife. In such situations—and we had several of them—the solution for the child's upbringing and education had to be found outside the township. Luckily, we had friends who had bought a farm in the mountains and out of the generosity of their hearts, were prepared to cater to just this kind of children in their school. Some other children are carrying the burden of having alcoholic parents. But, as so often happens in black communities, someone from the extended family will take them in.

Tetozo had considerable learning difficulties. By including the parents in searching for the right approach to help him, we learned that the man whom we thought was the rightful father had found this child as an abandoned baby in an alley. This is the most wonderful "social security" one can think of, that people take on the care and upbringing of children other than their own. Our experiences abound with such examples. Sometimes, like the case of Deliwe, children are tossed between members of the family. That makes a child insecure, as it does not really know where it belongs. In this special case, the better solution for Deliwe was to be with her grandmother. However, her grandmother was running a funeral parlor from her home and so the young girl had constant exposure to death and dying, which is too much to digest at such a young age.

Kgotatso, another child, was rescued by Theo from a disastrous

73

fate. When Theo saw him in the streets of Alexandra, he immediately recognized the child's potential. However, the boy was staying with his grandmother in an old shack. She had no money even to feed him, yet, whenever she had just a few rand, she would drown herself in booze. His father was in prison at that time and his mother had been shot by some rival "lover." The boy loves to come to school. Without it, he would sooner or later end up being a *tsotsi*.

More and more we also encounter the problem of sexual abuse of children as young as nursery school age. If sexual abuse occurs in the home, the mother usually has no other option than to remain in the home. Thus, she and her child have to stay where the abuse took place. These children really need a lot of attention and love to help them overcome their traumatic experiences.

We are trying to give special help with remedial lessons or with curative eurythmy, to which the children respond very well. Our child studies, trying to solve the riddle of just one child at a time, are astounding in their effects on the child. The mere fact that the whole college of teachers concentrates on the child in an objective, yet loving way, seems to help the child overcome seemingly insurmountable obstacles. The rich gifts of Waldorf education are subtle, yet very effective.

A new school gives unique opportunities to try new methods. As Sue, who came from Cape Town to help introduce a self-evaluation process for the teachers, wrote in her report: "This school is carried by an amazing amount of warmth, goodwill, and enthusiasm." To keep it on track, we must take conscious steps in all we do, in the interplay between the nursery and the primary school and in connection with the students who come to learn and to student teach in the classes. The challenges are enormous. The Baobab Centre has looked at this venture as a sort of pilot project, the first of its kind: the first Waldorf school in a township. We must constantly question ourselves. Whatever difficulties may exist, they must come out into the open, so they can be dealt with and remedied.

As the teachers college is responsible for running the school, teachers meetings that include study time, child studies, and artistic work for the further development of the teacher, can be very lengthy. It certainly is extremely demanding to be a Waldorf teacher. It asks of the teacher to be innovative, creative, nonjudgmental and, above all, to have a deep interest in children.

Discussions at regular intervals are necessary for renewal of commitment and setting of policies. We prefer to have our discussions in the natural setting of the African bush and therefore call them "Bush Indabas." (*Indaba* is the Zulu word for discussion.) Teachers can take their rightful place in class only if they know they are carried by the whole community of teachers.

Township Upheavals

The life of the school, as described before, is not a smooth ride. In 1990 we were very glad that the Inkanyezi school was left in peace when all the DET schools in Alexandra were constantly disrupted by teachers' strikes and marches to the DET headquarters. During 1991, however, the Inkanyezi school was much more affected because of the many fights and the violence taking place directly around the school.

Alexandra has three huge hostels for migrant laborers. An artificial division was made by the government, allocating two to men and one to women. In that way, each hostel housed people from different tribes which also meant people of different political persuasions. For years, these people had peacefully coexisted and had no intention of changing this because of instigators from the

outside. Then bands of armed black men started to appear in the townships. More and more they were seen as the "third force," people paid by those who wanted to disrupt the negotiation process and make the country ungovernable. The consequence was that hostel dwellers took up arms to fight those people invading the township. In the process, they became divided along ethnic lines. By that time, they were not only using the traditional weapons such as sticks and *pangas*, but they had guns as well.

The army of Red Bands, coming in from the outside, had declared the block of four streets just beyond the school to be their territory. Unbelievable tragedy ensued in terms of loss of life and burning of houses, especially shacks. In the end, killing became totally arbitrary. Bloodlust had taken over.

We lost children at our school when their entire family was brutally murdered. This particular family was not politically involved; yet, in the first clash the grandmother was killed. In the all-night vigil before her funeral, with all the relatives sitting or sleeping in a big tent erected outside the house as is customary for weddings and funerals, a group of men with AK47 rifles mowed down most of the relatives. Only those who were sleeping in the house survived the carnage. The grandfather, one of the survivors, lost his mind over this. Other family members took the children, who had miraculously survived, to a place in a rural area. For them, Alexandra was a place of death, never to return to. No one was ever apprehended; the mystery of this senseless killing was never solved.

With all these upheavals in the township, the teachers and parents developed a great sensitivity for the children's safety. They decided from day to day whether or not the children should come to school.

Sometimes, there were also false alarms. One day, Theo came to school to find a cardboard sign on the gate. It was signed "the Comrades," and ordered the school to close the whole of next week. Frankly, I was worried and thought this might be the beginning of an obstruction to our work. But Theo immediately decided to take the sign down. "If they want something of us," he said, "they better come and talk to us." The teachers display an amazing amount of courage. They constantly have to make decisions, weighing the safety of the children in their care against the potential disruption of the life of the school.

Most of the disruptions took place on weekends. For this

reason it was very difficult to have parents' meetings, as weekends were the only time they were able to attend a meeting. More than ever, we needed the parents' support, yet several times, the meetings had to be cancelled or stopped after only half an hour. Luckily, times of great upheaval alternate with more peaceful times during which one can concentrate again on the real task at hand: the education of the children for a better South Africa.

Parents Involvement

The ideal situation for children is to experience a unity between life at home and life at school. The child should not have to live in a divided world. It is therefore of utmost importance for the teachers to foster their connection with the parents. They should always feel that the teacher respects them for the large part they play in the upbringing and education of their children. Building bridges between home and school brings a feeling of trust and security into the child's life.

As not all teachers live in the township itself, it is even more essential that parents care not only about their children, but also about the school as a whole. A school needs the sheath of warmth it acquires through its caring parent body. But not only that. As indicated earlier, the Inkanyezi school wants to be a grassroots school. It does not want to ask exorbitant school fees from the parents, knowing that so many of them already have great difficulty paying the relatively low fees. Fortunately, many children have scholarships from overseas "godparents." The actual cost of running the school is much higher than can be covered by the monthly fees. We are privileged to have sister-schools in other countries making great efforts to send us a variety of necessary materials. Some of these school communities even earn money for Inkanyezi at their annual bazaars.

One school in the north of Germany stands out in its continued effort to support us. It is most helpful when teachers of those sister-schools can visit us and then transfer their impressions and enthusiasm to their pupils. In another school, situated in the industrial area of the northeastern part of Germany, almost each class has taken on one scholarship for a child of Inkanyezi. Through the increase of scholarships, it becomes ever more possible to let additional projects also benefit from this caring attitude of children at other Waldorf schools.

All Waldorf high schools in Scandinavia (Norway, Sweden, Denmark, Finland) have a program whereby several times a year the students pool the money they earn on behalf of Inkanyezi. This so impressed an agency from the Swedish government that it decided to offer substantial help for Baobab as well as for the planned craft workshops, i.e., metal and wood.

We are acutely aware of the immense value of such money given from the heart. However, the money from the students is given and needed for completion of the existing school building. The German government meanwhile is considering providing the Inkanyezi Children's Garden with its own building. The nursery school children urgently need a quieter, more secluded place with a playground and sandbox. At present, they are still housed in the primary school building that is filling up with each new class added every school year.

We are not sure how long this help from overseas will continue. With the founding of numerous Waldorf schools in the former East Bloc countries, resources are spread to help all the new initiatives. For this reason, it has been a fantastic offer from the developing Alexandra People's Organic Market to let our parents run the Tea Garden and allow the profits to go to the Inkanyezi school. Some coordinating efforts are needed, but there is a wonderful opportunity for parents to help raise funds for their children's education.

Each parent will be able to contribute something: ingredients for baking or cooking, preparing dishes or cakes to be sold, or giving some of their time to the school, by helping to run this Tea Garden. Or so we hoped. We did not realize how slow the start of the whole market was going to be when we asked the parents to volunteer time for the Tea House at the market. Nothing comes easily, especially not in a place like Alexandra, and many times we had to be very patient.

We realize that involving parents this way is quite unusual. In most other schools in South Africa, parents are kept at a distance and told not to interfere. We, on the other hand, ask them to become involved in a very concrete way. Active parent involvement is a concept of the international Waldorf school movement and has been practiced for more than seven decades on all levels of school life.

One can really see Waldorf schools as threefold socio-educational organisms consisting of the children, the parents, and the teachers.

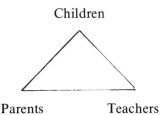

Children

Parents   Teachers

The Inkanyezi Waldorf Centre is operating under very difficult circumstances. It is still a young school operating with new concepts that, at first, are rather foreign to the parents. The healthy life of the school will, however, largely depend on input from the parents. The teachers are dedicated to their tasks, and the help of many parents will gradually make this a shared responsibility. The day will come when the Inkanyezi Centre will be run autonomously by the college of teachers in conjunction with an elected parent body. But before that, many other developments have yet to take place.

Festival Celebrations

We agree with the English historian Arnold Joseph Toynbee (1889-1975) that in the final analysis a civilization stands or falls with its ethical and spiritual values. That is why we felt our education had to touch what is deeply imbedded in the child's soul. Learning should be learning for life. Children, one day, will work in the world. They need to be equipped to fill their place in the world successfully and innovatively. Most of them will become parents themselves. Will they be equipped for parenthood? How about managing life itself with all its pitfalls and temptations? Will they have grown strong enough to deal with a changing world? Will they be swept away by the tides of change, or will they know who they are themselves? A really good education should prepare children for all aspects of life.

That is one reason so much emphasis is placed on art in Waldorf education. Also the religious education helps build a solid inner core in the child. Celebration of the festivals connects the child more intensively with the seasons of the year. As Inkanyezi is not only multiracial but also open to children of all religious denominations, these festivals can be Christian festivals as well as festivals important to the people of other faiths. Here

79

again lies an important link between the home and the school. If festivals are celebrated, they mostly happen in church. We, on the other hand, encourage parents to take up some of the ideas they witnessed by attending festivals at Inkanyezi and start celebrating them at home. It seems extremely important that real values be instilled at home. For example, when children bring their Advent lanterns and calendars home, they should be cherished and used as part of the Christmas festival celebrations in the home.

Advent, meaning the coming of Christmas, is celebrated in many countries four weeks before Christmas as a preparation for the birth of Christ. It is also celebrated in a special way at the Inkanyezi Children's Garden and Waldorf Centre. Four weeks before Christmas, the children of all three nursery groups at the Inkanyezi Children's Garden sat on their little chairs in a wide circle. In the middle of that circle, leading to a small mountain with a big burning candle on it, was a spiral path laid out with evergreen branches, decorated with beautiful minerals, flowers, and little gnomes. Each child, one by one, carried a candle set in an apple to the center of the circle, where the Christmas angel then helped it, if necessary, to light its own candle on the big Christmas light. While the children were walking in and out of the spiral form, soft music was played or the children themselves sang songs.

This special Advent celebration was initially introduced in 1920 by one of the teachers of the first Waldorf school in Stuttgart, Germany, and has been kept alive in the Waldorf schools throughout the world. Our nursery school teachers prepared the event so well that a mood of peace and harmony prevailed throughout. This was the best gift they could offer the children to take into their Christmas holidays.

Meanwhile, the students at the Waldorf Teacher Training Course had prepared a wonderful Christmas play for the children and parents. They had taken one of the well-known Oberuferer Christmas and Shepherds Plays, dating back to the late 16th or early 17th century, when they were performed in the town of Oberufer, Austria. These plays now are performed by Waldorf school teachers throughout the world as a present for the children every year at Christmastime. So did our teachers, having reworked one play with African songs, and changed in such a way that Alexandra became the setting of Christ's birth. The poverty, the worry about having to pay taxes, and the birth in a stable spoke directly to the hearts of the people in the audience.

After the play ended, darkness had fallen and all parents, guests, and children lit the candles they had brought and walked in a long procession through Alexandra. It was an unbelievable experience to see this courageous group of people, singing carols and carrying the light of Christmas through the township. Under normal circumstances one would have avoided going between the shacks but, because of the strong spirit of Christmas, this was undoubtedly the right thing to do. One of the old people from the Itlhokomeleng Old Age Home, along which the procession passed, expressed herself as follows:

Mostly, we are forgotten, but now you make us feel part of the whole of Alexandra again. This is the real Christmas spirit which will help to make Alexandra once more a place of hope.

Everybody requested that this would be made to happen every year. We all felt that the courage of the people was answered by the redemptive spirit of Christmas.

This procession took place in 1991. Christmas 1992 saw us again with an ever longer procession of candles. This time, many people, including the young, came out of their houses and shacks to join us and share the spirit of Christmas with the rest of the community at Alexandra.

CHAPTER IX

INITIATIVES IN SOWETO TOWNSHIP

Sikhulise Children's Garden in Soweto

In the teacher enrichment courses, held at Funda Centre in Soweto in 1986 and 1987, Mirriam (first mentioned in chapter 3) was the first to grasp the essence of the Waldorf education approach. She was also the first one wanting to bring this concept into her own community. Meadowlands, in Soweto, she said, was to get the benefit of such a wonderful education.

Mirriam worked in a DET school at the time. In a "bridging class" she cared for 45 children who need extra attention to prepare for the first class of primary school. They may be of the right school age, but never had stimulation either at home or at preschool, or they were just slower in their perceptions than the so-called "bright" children. Mirriam always had a wonderful way to further these children, but when she started to introduce what she had learned of Waldorf education in her class at the DET school, the children made such remarkable progress that the situation drew the attention of the inspector. From that time onward, Mirriam constantly had visitors in her class who observed how she worked.

Mirriam continued to work in the DET school. But in addition she started to look for suitable premises in Meadowlands to begin a Waldorf nursery school. She was fortunate to obtain permission from the Mahon Mission Church in Soweto to use their facilities. As Mirriam loved to share with neighbors, friends, or relatives what she had learned and understood, it was not difficult to attract a group of mostly young people who wanted to be trained as teachers. During an Easter holiday Mirriam was able to give these aspiring teachers a good foundation; together with these teachers-to-be, she invited a small group of children to her house. These training sessions brought Waldorf education to Soweto.

We were both happy and utterly amazed at how she tackled the training of her teachers. Every afternoon, after her own school day was over, she did in-service training with the new nursery school teachers. They would tell her about both the good things and the difficulties they had encountered during the day. After having advised them, Mirriam would then discuss the plans for the next day.

When we asked Mirriam in 1988 what she would like to call the new school in Soweto, we heard for the first time the name "Sikhulise Sun, Moon and Stars Children's Garden." Of course, the full name was soon dropped in everyday communication, but she was adamant that people's attention should be drawn to the heavenly bodies of the sun, the moon, and the stars. In Alexandra we had chosen *inkanyezi*, meaning star in Zulu, but she added the sun and the moon. The word *sikhulise* means upliftment in Zulu, and that is what Waldorf education, she hoped, would bring to the people. The teachers worked under Mirriam's supervision, and the number of children in the nursery school grew steadily, until a limit of 80 children was reached.

In the meantime, Mirriam had received an invitation by a Swedish friend of ours, who was deeply impressed by her work in Soweto, to come to Sweden for three months to the Waldorf Seminar in Stockholm and to visit different Waldorf schools in Sweden. Mirriam received much inspiration on that trip, but she also gave a lot of herself wherever she went. After coming back, she was more than ever convinced that this was the educational model for the future. She was also touched by eurythmy, the art of movement, taught as part of the curriculum in all Waldorf schools. By doing eurythmy every day it had become a real experience for her. She felt that kind of artistic movement was especially important for black people, as it would free them from being so earthbound.

Meanwhile, the teachers at Sikhulise were coping as best they could. But working with 80 children in a small church was not easy. Although the teachers received very low salaries, they decided they should contribute toward the acquisition of a prefabricated hut to accommodate a group of older children.

The people of Meadowlands are quite underprivileged and the parents were hard pressed to pay the R 35 tuition per month. More and more young people were attracted to join the teaching staff, not for financial gain, but because they felt the good spirit present in the nursery school and looked for a meaningful occupation.

One of those teachers was Queen. She had been with Sikhulise for a while, when an opportunity arose to study Waldorf education at the Novalis College in Cape Town. For several years, Novalis College offered a one-year Foundation Year and a one-year Waldorf Teacher Training program under the auspices of Novalis Institute in Cape Town. The Novalis Institute for Adult Education was established in 1989 and concerns itself with outreach projects. Baobab Centre, with the help of a grant from the Australian Embassy, had already been able to send two people to Novalis College. With Queen going to Cape Town for training, a real possibility arose of starting a Waldorf school in Soweto upon her return.

Mirriam was often extremely worried about the developments in Soweto's educational arena. The DET teachers took the reigns, pushing the school principals aside and dictating the ways for all other teachers. Mirriam belonged to a specific teachers' organization. The teachers belonging to another very politically oriented teachers' organization suddenly decided that there was only going to be one teachers' organization, namely theirs. According to their philosophy, power lay in unity. Therefore, they used intimidation tactics to force all teachers over to their side.

At the end of 1991, Mirriam risked her life and her home by standing up and saying that she had enough of being bulldozed into things she did not believe in. They all had suffered under the domination of the DET and its inspectors and now things were turning even worse. If they had the courage, they should come and kill her or burn down her house. With that, she gave them her address.

That evening, Mirriam sent away all her family members and sat alone at home, waiting for the worst to happen. Fortunately, all her friends and relatives came to her and together they prayed that reason might prevail and that the radical teachers would not harm her. Nothing happened—but such is life in Soweto: one has to be careful always to speak softly. People live in such close proximity that intimidation, supposedly for a good purpose, is rampant.

After all these troubles, Mirriam initiated yet a Saturday morning school. On the one hand, she wanted more children to have the benefit of at least some exposure to Waldorf education; on the other, she was preparing the ground for the Sikhulise Children's Garden to grow into a full Waldorf primary school.

The start of Inkanyezi in Alexandra had been difficult enough and wrought with disappointments. To begin something in Soweto seemed even more difficult. Over long periods, Mirriam suggested that we, as white people, should not show our faces. Her reasoning was that parents would become passive, expecting the whites to do everything for them, or the comrades would torpedo the initiative because whites were connected with it.

At a certain moment we felt that it was important for the teachers to feel our support. It had been clear from the beginning in all our dealings with the *Isigodi Segolide* projects (Zulu for golden circles described in chapter 16) that arose from the Baobab Centre that each initiative was autonomous and independent. But we also had to be ready to stand by and offer suggestions in areas of fund-raising, bookkeeping, community development, and further training.

Besides all the activity connected with being a class teacher, nurturing the new Sikhulise initiative and holding a Saturday morning school, Mirriam undertook another major task. She had a diploma as a preschool teacher that enabled her to teach the bridging class, which she had been doing for years. In view of all the developments toward a Waldorf primary school, she felt she should have a regular teachers certificate from the DET Teachers Training College. This meant attending the college four after-noons a week and doing homework in the evenings. It was certainly extremely important that she did this course, but it was taxing her strength to the limit.

Venus Children's Garden in Soweto

Surely, it is clear by now that Mirriam is a deeply caring person. At times, she tried to protect herself from too many people coming to her for advice. Yet, if she thought she could help or create a situation where more children could have access to Waldorf education, she would instantly forget about her own needs and be there for the community. In 1991, the Methodist Church—located in Meadowlands along with the Sikhulise Children's Garden—offered Mirriam use of the church for an offshoot of Sikhulise.

Three teachers from Sikhulise were prepared to try and develop this initiative. In line with the name Sikhulise Sun Moon and Stars Children's Garden, they called it the Venus Children's Garden, as Venus is the planet of love, and that would be the appropriate name for this nursery school. They traveled a bumpy road, not the least because the enrollment was low for a long time. But now, a proud group of "survivors" told us that they have 36 children and a solid parent committee. One must admire those people who carry on serving a worthy cause when even their most basic needs are not met.

The Beginning of a Waldorf Primary School in Soweto

By the middle of 1991, when it was clear that Queen (of whom we spoke earlier) definitely wanted to be the teacher of the first Waldorf primary class in Soweto, Mirriam, together with some parents, started to look actively for a site for the new school.

Meantime, Mirriam started to teach in a TED school in Johannesburg. That school had just become multiracial. Previously, the TED schools (Transvaal Education Department) only admitted white children. However, since 1992, the parent body of each TED school was permitted to decide whether or not the school should become multiracial. It was in one such school that Mirriam began to teach. Simultaneously, she and her friends continued their search for space in Soweto. Of course, they needed permission from the Soweto Town Council, and for that reason Mirriam sought the assistance of the mayor of Soweto.

One day in 1992, Mirriam called us, devastated: "The mayor has been assassinated." Just before his death, he had visited Sikhulise, was very impressed, and promised his assistance in getting a site for the school. Such are the unbelievable setbacks one has to deal with in South Africa at the present time.

Much time will have to pass before Mirriam can again approach the Town Council. Life in most of South Africa is completely politicized. Neutrality is not supposed to exist. One is either on this side of the political spectrum or on the other.

Therefore, at least for the time being, the best solution was that class I of the primary school would start in the Zozo hut (a South African trademark name for a prefabricated hut) that had been acquired to accommodate the older children at the Sikhulise Children's Garden. Of course, it is a setback for the Children's Garden to again have only one space in the church for all the children. But on the other hand, it seems a great asset to have the whole Waldorf project together in one location. Under the circumstances described so far, it would be quite unthinkable to have one lonely class with one teacher out on a limb.

Queen has had two years of training at Novalis College in Cape Town. It was remarkable how that time away from Soweto changed her outlook on life. The radiant sunlike nature of her being, no doubt, will shine ever more abundantly on "the little angels," as she calls the children in her charge. So far, eight couples have committed themselves to the primary school, this new venture. They are the brave, pioneering spirits like those first parents of the Inkanyezi Waldorf Centre in Alexandra. Inkanyezi also started with eight children, and today the teachers there constantly have to disappoint parents by turning children away, because the number of children per class needs to be restricted to about 45, so that quality education may be upheld and enough attention given to each individual child.

It was reasonable to expect a similar development at Sikhulise. And, indeed, it began. In January 1993, a new first class of the primary school began with Nicki, Lorna's sister, as class teacher. As the Mahon Mission Church did not want another Zozo hut on their premises, the one prefab originally intended for one class had to be divided so it could be used for two classes. Though struggling financially, the seed is growing stronger and stronger.

High fees cannot be expected from the parents in Meadowlands, because they struggle to make ends meet. Queen and Nicki are prepared to put themselves totally behind the school, but cannot yet concern themselves with fund-raising. At the moment, it is more important for them to continue their training at Baobab and to have time for their own in-service training.

Mirriam has two more years ahead of her before she will obtain her teaching certificate. With all her involvement it is impossible for her to spend time fundraising. All we can hope, therefore, is that the watchful guardian spirit of the school will motivate the right people at the right moment to support this first Waldorf school in Soweto.

Eric, one of the Baobab trainers, visits the school regularly and works with the teachers' college to help the school off to a good start. In the meantime, the search for a proper school site has continued. As a result, a new community centre not far from the Mahon Church has been found. It had been vandalized by the youth for political reasons. Once restored, the building could become the ideal place for the Sikhulise Waldorf School. It also would mean the redemption of a very negative act of violence. In

addition to the purchase price of land and building, restoration of
the building itself will be costly.

Is the Sikhulise Waldorf School ready for this big leap into the
unknown? There is hope based on our experience of being faced
with the impossible from the beginning of our work and not only
surviving but thriving. We expect some financial help from
Sweden where Mirriam's visit generated great interest in her work.

The seeds for further development have been sown. For now,
the most important thing is the care and education of the children
and the development of a caring parent body. The path is open to
those who have the means to help promote such a promising new
beginning.

CHAPTER X

THE INITIATIVE IN SHARPEVILLE TOWNSHIP

Inkanyezi Children's Garden in Sharpeville

Sharpeville is a township one-and-a-half hours' drive south of Johannesburg. There, another seedling of the Baobab tree is growing. In 1987, it was planted by Zodwa, who is nurturing it at her own home.

Zodwa heard about Waldorf education for the first time from Dudu. Dudu had already grasped the importance of this new educational approach, so much so, that she enrolled Khanyo, her daughter, at the Michael Mount Waldorf School in Bryanston, one of Johannesburg's suburbs. In 1987, Dudu arranged for Zodwa to visit the Inkanyezi Children's Garden in Alexandra when it was still at the Mahon Mission Church.

Zodwa clearly saw all that needed more development, but she also saw those beautiful ideas in action. She already had a small crèche at her own house in Sharpeville, but because of having taken a longer study break, she had lost the children in her care. In 1988, with renewed enthusiasm, fired by the ideas of a truly child-centered education, Zodwa started once more with a group of children in her garage.

This place was not specially suited for the purpose, but confronted with the choice of having one's child in the care of a warm-hearted person or having no place at all for that child, parents would look beyond the outer appearance and be pleased to enroll their child at her child care, named the Inkanyezi Children's Garden after the Alexandra initiative.

What made the parents decide was that Zodwa was all heart and soul for the children. Her task was not to be only a nursery school teacher, as some children were brought to her already at 5 a.m. Having to be at work at 8 a.m., and having to travel two hours to get to work, parents have no choice but to deliver their children

at the crèche as early as 5 a.m. The same holds true at the end of the day, when parents again need to travel two hours to reach home. Thus, the days are very long, indeed, for the children as well as Zodwa. She has to fulfill the role of mother or grandmother, because the children are with her for so many hours.

At Inkanyezi in Sharpeville, the parents also paid minimal fees. From this money, Zodwa had to feed the children all day. Part of the life of the nursery school took place in her house: she cooked in her kitchen and the 25 children used her toilet. Zodwa knew that it was not ideal, but it was a way to get started. Neither was it ideal that the children should have only a small section of concrete— her driveway—for playing. She used newspaper as tablecloth. The few toys were donations originally given to Baobab.

Soon Zodwa actively tried to raise funds to enlarge the garage space. And she was successful! With money from the U.S. Embassy, she was able to extend her garage and even build toilets. Now, at last, she would be able to increase the number of children to 45. But, at that point in time, all kinds of disasters hit the township of Sharpeville.

It started with the trial of the "Sharpeville Six." During a riot in

90

the township a big crowd had gathered to vent their anger about the ongoing collaboration of the town councillors with the apartheid regime. The crowd marched to the house of one of the councillors. The result was that the councillor was murdered, actually lynched. The police brought six people to trial who had been part of the crowd. Those six men had been at the back of the crowd and were definitely not directly involved in the killing. Still, all six were charged with murder and were to get the death penalty.

Zodwa told us of the continuous prayer meetings she was attending, because she knew the family of one of the six young men. The court trials stretched out for months and it was a difficult period for Sharpeville. In the end, the sentences of the six were commuted to life sentences. And, later still, they were released in exchange for the release of some political activists from the Afrikaner Resistance Movement (AWB).

Once this traumatic happening was over, the "taxi killings" in nearby Sebokeng started. The taxi (minibus transport) business is the most lucrative of black businesses and highly competitive. The fight is in fact about territorial claims. Taxi owners take the law into their own hands, resulting in numerous killings. The taxi war flared up again and again in several parts of the country. In many places, such as Gugulethu and Khayelitsha in Cape Province, where the Baobab Centre was active, a similar taxi war has been raging for a long time. There, rivalry over the rights to operate on a certain route became so strong that taxi owners were ready to wage a war and kill each other in the process.

Life on the streets of Sharpeville was very dangerous. Often people did not dare go to work, even if that meant losing their jobs. Thus, it was also too dangerous to bring the children to the nursery school. When all those troubles finally ceased, electricity to Sharpeville was cut off as a consequence of the rent boycotts. Zodwa had to cook on wood and coal outside the house and could not use the electrical heaters to keep the children warm during cold winter months.

All of this sounds like a tale of disaster—and that is exactly what it was. Each time I spoke with Zodwa on the telephone, she would sigh deeply, relate the latest disaster and, at the same time, say: "But I will continue to carry the torch!"

All the women about whom I have spoken are exceptional human beings. They need all the help they can possibly get from those who realize how important these educational initiatives are.

The education of South African children has to be rebuilt from scratch.

At a meeting of all the *Isigodi Segolide* initiatives arising from the Baobab Centre, we heard how, finally, the tide seems to be turning for Zodwa. Several parents had taken their children to multiracial nursery schools, as that seemed to be the in thing to do. Soon they realized the advantages of the Waldorf approach to education Zodwa had given their children in contrast to the education their children were receiving at the government school. Many parents came back and begged her to take their child again.

This resulted in Zodwa having a committed group of parents who want to see the Inkanyezi Children's Garden flourish and develop into a Waldorf primary school. They are prepared to make sacrifices so their children may receive this kind of education. Enrollment has again gone up to 34 and many more parents are expected to awaken to the fact that Inkanyezi-Sharpeville has something essential to offer their children. Although many disasters have struck her, Zodwa holds fast to her dreams of having a piece of land on which to build a nursery school and, later, a Waldorf primary school.

We feel so connected with Zodwa and her good impulse, yet, it was so difficult to keep up contact. Sharpeville has constantly been in the news because of all the violence that happened in and around the township. We kept trying to contact Zowdwa by phone but for some reason hers had been cut off. I wrote to her three times but never received a reply. My colleagues at the Baobab Centre tried to convince me to give up on Zodwa, but I could not. So I finally wrote one more letter to tell her that I was going to be overseas for a while. How amazed was I, after arriving in the Netherlands, to find an express letter waiting for me. It was from Zodwa. She had sent it at great expense, considering her small income. She asked never to give up on her and to understand that her problems and the situation in the township were so extremely difficult that at times she was unable to stay in active contact with us. She wrote that if she wants to go anywhere she has to have a comrade accompany her and she even has to pay his bus fare. This is the way the comrades control the township and everybody living in it. Yet, she carries on and wants to be one of the golden circles of *Isigodi Segolide.*

CHAPTER XI

INDIVIDUALITY AND COMMUNITY

The healthy social life is found
when in the mirror of each human soul
the whole community finds its reflection
and when in the community
the virtue of each one is living.

Rudolf Steiner
Verses and Meditations

The gift from the African people to the world is their strong social conscience. "The community" is the magic word. It is the coherence between people. An African saying is: "A person is something only because of another person." There is much truth in that.

One example in Alexandra township is Itlhokomeleng Old Age Home. It is a very special place in that it is the first old age home for black people in South Africa that is run as a welfare organization and has been registered by a black person, Marjorie Manganye, whose name was already mentioned in chapter 6.

When black people get older, they mostly stay with family. But it also happens in this strange South African world that people lose touch with their families. This can easily happen when fathers and mothers have to work elsewhere. One of the ladies at Itlhokomeleng Old Age Home told me she worked as a domestic for white people for 50 years. She cared for the white children of her employer while having to neglect her own. This is very common.

In the trial of a terrorist in South Africa, the young man who had thrown a bomb in a shopping center and in the end repented his deed, explained how anger had built up in him when he grew up knowing that his mother neglected him in favor of the white children. This jealousy had eaten away his inner core and the only way he knew to vent his anger was to lash out in a deed of violence against the white world.

Itlhokomeleng Old Age Home indeed is a community of very lonely, lost people. Seldom does a visitor come to see any of the old people. In their youth, the children seldom have seen their mothers; they lived in separation, and now the children are strangers to their parents.

At the home, the old people are housed in such a way that two share a prefabricated hut. There is just enough room for two beds with a narrow passage in between. On a nail on the wall they hang their few articles of clothing.

Outside are a few crude, backless benches; often the people of the home are sitting or half hanging on their beds. Through a donation by friends in Holland we were able to buy each of them a simple folding chair. Imagine the day shortly before Christmas 1986, when we unpacked the cartons and to their great surprise out came the colorful chairs. We put all 28 of them outside in the yard in a big circle. The people have no other place where they can sit together, as there are no larger rooms available, not even for meals. So this was a major event, having everyone sitting together outside in a circle. More than anything else, it was a social event and we celebrated it by singing together.

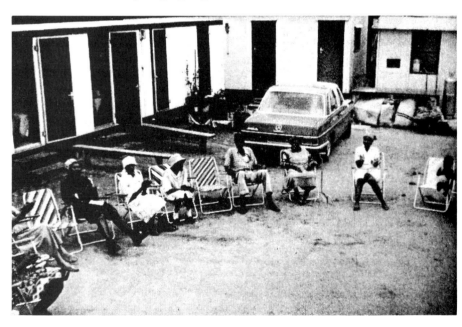

Later, we heard it took a lot of persuasion from the director of the home to convince the people they now could throw away the old tins they used for chairs. The people were not used to such beautiful new things, they would rather have continued to use the old tins. But, finally, they let themselves be convinced that it was all right to use the new chairs.

If enough funds can be obtained, the committee in charge of Itlhokomeleng plans to build a real Old Age Home with a dining room for all, a place for entertainment, and for occupational activities. The idea is to have a nursery for children on the grounds so that the old people feel connected with the community and especially with young children.

It is a miracle that the masses of people who are unemployed, and for whom there is no welfare system, are surviving. Very often one person from an extended family, which is usually very large, is the sole bread winner. It is expected that this one person provide for all. Even though families are already big they will, nevertheless, take in children of relatives who died. But not only children of relatives. In the Inkanyezi school are numerous examples of parents taking children into their homes, regardless of whether or not they are related. Often, teenagers who are still attending school have babies. It is amazing how such a happening is handled and taken on as a responsibility by the whole family. The main point is that the girl goes back to school. If we would ask black people the question, "Are you your brother's keeper?" most of them would look at you with big eyes and answer: "Of course we are."

Another example of the community factor are funerals. I myself was present at the funeral of Seda, who was one of our first doll makers. As she was old and walked with crutches, she mostly sat quietly in her room at the old age home in Alexandra, happy to make dolls. Seldom did she have a visitor. She had lost contact even with her children. In her younger years, she had been a cook in Soweto. Now she found herself at Itlhokomeleng Old Age Home, somewhat lost and lonely.

How amazed was I to see two big busses full of people arrive at Seda's funeral. In this absolutely dismal graveyard, stretching as far as the eye could see, with only little mounds covered with ordinary stones or pieces of concrete, a most amazing spectacle unfolded. The crowd present was enormous; the funeral service and the speeches about Seda's life were constantly interspersed with the most beautiful singing. It was not the burial of a lonely pauper, it was the burial of a queen! The community, mostly from the church in Soweto to which she belonged, had not forgotten her!

And here is another example: In all our Baobab workshops we always had an array of people ranging from those who were illiterate to those who had traveled the world and gone to universities. Yet, everybody respected each other for what they were. It is this feeling of humility prevailing among black people that brings about the attitude "every person is somebody, because he is a child of God." Countless additional examples could be related.

So far, I indicated the life-saving quality of the community spirit, a quality that made it possible to survive the most horrendous attacks on the lives and spirit of the black people, who not merely survived but survived with grace and dignity.

There are still other sides to the community spirit. Whenever decisions have to be taken, the process is extremely slow. People who attend meetings are there, because they have the mandate to attend that meeting. All they can do is listen and take back to their community what they have heard. Being democratic in such a way makes it hard to come to decisions.

It also makes it difficult to be innovative. In most members of the community lives the conviction that the old ways are the best and the oldest people have the greatest wisdom.

Of course, one could ask oneself what constitutes the community: the enlarged family, the tribe, the elders, the village, the political party, the African community as a whole, or the totality of humanity? Where is there place for the individual? Has the individual the right to be different? Rugged individualism can be a grand illusion, but so can a onesided emphasis on community.

Europe, and especially America, have gone overboard with the emphasis on the individual. Not for nothing was the American generation of the 1970s and 1980s called the "me" generation. Martin Luther King Jr. (1929-1986), leader of the Human Rights movement in America and advocate of nonviolence, represented the deeper, underlying current of black Americans who, as Americans, had also joined this "me" generation, when he said to them:

> An individual has not started living until he can rise above the narrow confines of his individualistic concerns to the broader concerns of all humanity.[12]

Or,

Every man must decide whether he will walk in the light of creative altruism or in the darkness of destructive selfishness. This is the judgment. Life's most persistent and urgent question is: What are you doing for others?[13]

Across the world, nationalism is rearing its head. That is understandable. People of different languages and cultures have been oppressed and deprived of their identity for centuries. Before arriving at the bigger concept of belonging to the world community, they will first have to find their own identity.

In South Africa alone, people from different ethnic backgrounds are living and working together in all townships. It is absolutely astounding how they manage to handle the complex language aspects, for example. On the continent of Africa, the diversification of languages is greater than anywhere else in the world. With that has grown the ability of black people to cope. It is no exception to meet Africans who speak about 10 different languages. Most people, including children, speak at least three or four. And these languages are quite different from each other.

Much of what people overseas read or see on TV about the division of South Africans along ethnic lines, has been manipulated by different groups under the motto "divide and rule."

Yes, black people should be aware of their ethnic traditions. But that does not mean they should be imprisoned by them. Yes, children should be exposed to the roots of their heritage, but as they grow up, they should develop the same respect for the heritage of other people. As Arthur Schlesinger Jr. wrote:

The United States of America escaped the divisiveness of a multiethnic society by the creation of a new national identity.[14]

South Africa is in the process of creating a new identity for all in the "new South Africa" or, as other people would put it, in a "better South Africa." Though this might become a new identity, it would still be a national identity.

The world is a whole, an entity, even though countries are divided and have borders. Africa, including South Africa, needs the world. For far too long, South Africa was cut off from the world community. Now it is reaching out and longing for recognition by the world. If the world's interest is limited only to the economic level, it will not be good enough.

Africa and South Africa have a tremendous gift to offer the world—the gift of social renewal! Whenever people come together, at meetings, at weddings, at funerals, etc., they go through the most astonishing rituals. African people, as a matter of course, take time for these things. Culture without ritual can be compared to the emperor without clothes, and can hardly be called a "real" culture.

How, then, can culture renew itself? By creating new rituals. Professor Harriet Ngubane (Professor of Anthropology at the University of the Western Cape) went as far as to say that the only bridge for black people to comfortably enter the white world would be through creation of new rituals. In other words, human egohood—the bare core of our existence—must find new clothes (new rituals) to cover its nakedness. At the same time, the community can find its renewal only through the diversified responses of its individuals. Rollo May, the American psychologist, expresses it this way:

> The future lies with the man or woman, who can live as an individual conscious within the solidarity of the human race. He then uses the tension between individuality and solidarity as the source of his ethical creativity.[15]

The solution lies in learning consciously to live with the flow between the individual and the community. We cannot be social beings if we do not know who we are as individuals. But we can discover who we really are only when we engage ourselves socially with the life of the community.

In her article "Living into Africa,"[16] the physician Susan Arstall describes how it was customary in some tribes to punish a wrongdoer by having him stand alone in the center of a circle formed by all the villagers.

Another interesting experience I had, when making mandala[17] drawings with a mixed group of white and black people, was the task of drawing oneself in picture form in connection with the community. The black people drew themselves as one of the bubbles in the big community bubble. The white people made all kinds of different mandala forms, but with one thing in common, their own center as a point rather than a bubble and firmly rooted in the center of the whole picture.

Only that attitude of life that is flexible enough to combine the two extremes in a flowing, living way, bears the potential for a peaceful future for us all. I think we can speak with Ingoapele Madingoane who says: "I must define the value of humanity to myself and the value of myself to humanity."[18]

CHAPTER XII

THE RURAL AREAS OF SOUTH AFRICA

Educating Children of Farmworkers in Natal

Education of black children in the rural areas depends on the initiative of the white farmers. If they are prepared to put up the buildings for a school, the DET will pay half of the cost of the buildings.

In the 1980s, Nino and Diana Rivera started their biodynamic farm, employing the biodynamic agricultural methods that work in a healing way with the earth, near Estcourt in Natal, a five-hour drive from Johannesburg, they were soon approached with the request to start a farm school. It was important to the Riveras that this school should become a school based on Waldorf educational principles. With a minimum of cost they were able to build a beautiful school with many windows and painted in bright colors. It was called Meadowsweet Farm School.

Claartje and I agreed to introduce the principal and teachers of this farm school to the Waldorf educational ideas. Because the drive from Johannesburg is so long, we managed to go there only

one weekend every month. The first year we mainly worked with the teachers of the school at the Riveras' farm plus one additional school, later the number of participating schools increased.

We always spent one morning teaching the children of the farm school ourselves, so the teachers could witness Waldorf education in action. Mrs. Hlongwane, the principal of the farm school and her teachers worked in such a way with the children that, as a result of the training sessions, the walls of the classrooms were soon adorned with watercolor paintings and drawings.

This display made it possible to see the development of the children from month to month. Initially, the drawings were stiff and bare, but slowly they gained more life and color and became more expressive. The children also started to feel free to greet us and to answer questions. The Waldorf educational approach opened new avenues in the souls of the children who are extremely shy, especially in the rural areas.

The teachers from another farm school in that same area had no cooperation from the farmer. They had to teach under very difficult circumstances with two classes sitting back to back in one space with a badly leaking roof, with wind and rain having free play, and such small windows that one could hardly see anything. For this reason it was even more remarkable how the teachers and their principal maintained a wonderful attitude and were able to create something positive for the children, in spite of these difficult cirumstances.

We were amazed how, at this other farm school, Mavis, teaching the combined first and second grades, with 70 children in two separate rooms, was able to implement all she had learned with us and create a real Waldorf class atmosphere in the midst of such negativity and devastating poverty. After many years of also working with handicapped children, Mavis is now a teacher at Meadowsweet Farm School and, as ever, a shining light in that capacity.

Meadowsweet Farm School is under its own trust, the Nkonjane Trust. In that sense it is not directly part of the Baobab initiatives. Yet, we have strong ties with Meadowsweet and the Riveras as many of our students are able to do their student teaching at the farm school. Two of our students, Bongani and Thulani, who started their training with Baobab in 1991, are now successful class teachers at Meadowsweet.

Meadowsweet began as a strong farm school and over time it

became even stronger. It even started a high school, which is exceptional for a farm school. Astonishingly, the government, paying the teachers' salaries, is permitting the teachers to work with the Waldorf educational ideas.

Rural Customs

In the black homelands of South Africa, the situation is quite different. Since some of the *Isigodi Segolide* initiatives derived from the activity of the Baobab Centre for Teacher Enrichment spread into two black homelands in Northern Transvaal, we experienced some of the customs in those rural areas.

In general we may say that before white people appeared, black communities lived in harmony with their environment and practiced a highly differentiated cultural life, firmly grounded in sound social structures. How, for example, did people cope with years of drought? They built deep, wide chambers far below the earth's surface, with a narrow entrance large enough for a person to enter. The walls of the chamber were first covered with a certain kind of wet clay, after which a big fire was lit, baking the clay and thus insulating the inside from heat, humidity, and insects. Usually, this chamber was built underneath the floor of the cattle kraal, because that is a sacred place and also because fresh manure is the best protection against disease. In these chambers enough food could be stored to keep the village community from starving during times of drought.

How did people wash their hair before shampoo was introduced to them? Emily told us:

Today, young people think they can't wash their hair without shampoo. We never had shampoo, but we did wash our hair regularly. We just went out to get a certain little plant. By touching it with a wet hand, we would already feel the soapiness of it. It was perfect. We did not need anything else.

Another wonderful example of how people coped, at least in certain rural areas, was the way they received a newborn baby into their midst. First of all, they were convinced the baby's first months should be quiet and without any major upheavals. Thus, for three months, the mother stayed with the baby, at first in the rondavel (round hut) and then within the limits of the small compound around the house. At three months, the village community prepared itself to receive the newborn child into its midst. But how can a child be received if there are still bad feelings and grudges amongst the people? Should not the new earthling be received into a community free of grievances? And so, all people would come together, wearing ropes with one or more knots around their waists. One by one, they would come forward, and while undoing the knots in the rope, would reveal what kind of knots of jealousy, hatred, or ill-feelings they still carried in their soul. Only after all had bared their souls and a cleansing process had healed all community wounds, could the newborn be received. This is a most extraordinary custom and one from which white people can learn.

One more example of an African custom that may seem far removed from our understanding is the following. The healers, diviners or sangomas (witch doctors) are, to this day, "throwing the bones," to read the future and to understand the causes of illness. The bones of goats are used. "Why goats?" My friends were amazed that I should ask such a dumb question. "Of course, bones of goats," they said, "are they not grazing everywhere, in everybody's yard, around everybody's hut? If they don't know all the secrets, who then would know?"

How can one reconcile the true values of the past—many of which are alive to this day in rural areas—with late 20th century realities?

The situations just described concern those people who, under the apartheid system, were allowed to stay on the land. Although the black people of South Africa outnumber whites by seven to one, they were apportioned only 13% of the land and of that often those parts least arable and lacking natural resources. One project I will describe later on, is situated in Venda, a semihomeland in the far northern Transvaal. The so-called "homelands" are areas allocated partly along ethnic lines and partly along economic lines to all those not directly needed to work for the whites.

Indirectly, the independent states were also affected by the government's decision, but the homelands were a direct consequence of keeping people of color apart in separate areas. To this day, the reality is that all able-bodied men go to work in the factories and mines and the women work mainly as domestics, so only small little children and old people are left in the villages. Some women may stay at home, provided their husbands are faithful and send them money.

It is not an easy commitment to keep a marriage intact when one realizes that men only see their families, at best, once a month, or, if the distance is too great and the travel expences too high, once a year at Christmas. And that condition prevails year after year. Many husbands lose their jobs, others get ill or are involved in accidents. Many died in the many clashes in the townships, which are always concentrated around the hostels. All of a sudden, a woman is faced with a complete loss of income. What is she to do? The only alternative is to leave her children with older family members and try to find work in the city.

How does a community sustain itself under such circumstances? It is the custom of many black people living far from home to stay actively involved with the well-being of their communities. For instance, at the beginning of 1989, representatives of the Baobab Centre had the opportunity to meet with 12 male relatives of Emily's extended family while she was in England for further training. Those meetings took place at the men's hostel in Alexandra. We discussed how Emily could realize her dream of starting a Waldorf school in Madietane in the homeland of Lebowa and how the men could liaise between the chief and the Baobab Centre's trainers.

Of course, there are scores of people who were forcibly removed from their ancestral land and dumped in arid places, having to live with total strangers who had suffered the same fate. Such places, ironically, or rather cynically, received such names as Compensation, in Natal. Another example was Sophiatown, in Johannesburg. After all the people were uprooted and removed from what was once a vibrant township in Johannesburg, where people of all races lived together, the new name, chosen for the now "for whites only" suburb was Triomf!

And now that the pass-laws, forcing blacks to carry passes and restricting their freedom of movement, are a thing of the past and people are free to go where they want, the flight from the land has taken on enormous proportions. Millions of people live around the big cities in shacks erected of cardboard or corrugated iron, or even under plastic sheets, always hoping to find work. At the same time, campaigns are waged to convince people to go back and hold on to the land, because that is still better than the nothingness they face in the slums of shacks.

As our experience has shown, there is still community support functioning in rural areas. This became evident when Waldorf projects were started in the homeland of Lebowa, as well as in the homeland of Venda, both in Northern Transvaal.

CHAPTER XIII

INITIATIVES IN THE HOMELAND OF LEBOWA

A Woman Called Emily and Her Dream

What endures?
Nothing endures but personal qualities.
A great city is that which has the greatest men and women.
If it be a few rugged huts,
it is still the greatest city on earth.

Walt Whitman
Leaves of Grass

When we began training people for the Inkanyezi Children's Garden in Alexandra in 1986, Emily took the opportunity to participate. Throughout her adult life she had to work in Johannesburg away from Madietane, a village in the homeland of Lebowa in Northern Transvaal where she grew up. Of her three children, only the eldest was a few years with her. The others spent most of their school life in boarding schools, seeing their mother only once a month or during Christmas holidays.

Emily was deeply attached to her home community. Her one wish was to be able to go back one day and help uplift her people. When we began training nursery school teachers, Emily saw this as a real chance for receiving the necessary training and skills so she could go back to her village and help her people. It was clear to her after her training that she would still need to gain practical experience with children in a nursery school setting. Thus, for two years, Emily helped with the Inkanyezi Children's Garden in Alexandra. She was completely committed to the well-being of the children, and carried her part of the responsibilities for the project with great steadfastness.

It is interesting to mention that Emily had come into contact with Waldorf education early in her life. It happened that since the

1960s she had worked for many years as a domestic servant in David and Betty's house. This family decided to start a Waldorf nursery school in their own garage. Emily's child was the only black child in that nursery school.

Although Emily was not directly involved with that nursery school, she nevertheless absorbed a whole new way of dealing with small children. It appealed to her. She also felt that her son had received a true foundation upon which to build his life. It is quite possible that her wish to one day begin a nursery school in her home village was born then and there. But she still had to wait some 30 years until the time was ripe for such an undertaking.

Her employers—who also happen to be good friends of ours— saw that Emily had capabilities way beyond those of a domestic servant and encouraged her to go to evening school.

She already had a matriculation certificate. To convey an impression of the determination of this woman, one has to understand that to go to high school from her village, while still in her teens, she had to walk each day for four hours to get there and, obviously, another four hours home again. That meant leaving her village at 4 a.m. and returning at 7 p.m. She had no shoes and no coat to wear and only one dress. Her path led over the mountains where she had to face baboons that could at times be aggressive. All day long, she went without food. And these were only some of the conditions she had to deal with if she wanted to get a matriculation certificate.

While a domestic servant, Emily was able to take evening classes in business and bookkeeping. After successfully completing the courses, she was eager to start, at last, in a job that would provide a better income. But, ironically, under the apartheid regime she had a permit to be in Johannesburg for work as a domestic servant but not in any other job and nothing could be done about it, even though she had the qualifications to do different work. This again was one of the many severe setbacks she had to face in her life.

However, she did not give up and kept pursuing all possible avenues. Then, one day, it was finally possible to be hired by a business in Johannesburg. Because of her outstanding qualities, she was soon promoted to department manager. Then she heard that she was to be stationed in Spain to promote her firm's business in that country.

But, once again, life dealt Emily a blow: Betty, the woman in whose household she had been working for many years, died, leaving behind several small children. In desperation, David, the widower, asked Emily to come back to the family and be a mother for his children. It is almost impossible to comprehend the loyalty Emily displayed in deciding her future. A new life was opening up for her with wonderful opportunities to earn a good salary and see the world. Yet, out of the goodness of her heart, she chose to return to her previous employer and take up the task of being a mother to his children. Once again, she was one of the countless black mothers in South Africa caring for white children, while her own children were deprived of their mother's care.

Pauline, David's second wife, (who was mentioned in chapter 5) was working with us from the beginning. In fact, she had the connection to Alexandra. When the idea of training teachers for a nursery school in Alexandra came about, Pauline suggested that Emily take part. Emily took this opportunity with both hands. When we met Emily at the end of the 1980s, her children had grown up. At long last, she could follow the call of her heart and return to her community after having gained sufficient training.

To some extent, David and Pauline rewarded Emily by organizing funds for her to go to England for a three-month training period in 1989. She was in a Waldorf nursery school in the mornings and partook in the training course in the afternoons. She also saw that private school initiatives in England were struggling financially and that poor white people, indeed, existed.

While in England, Emily was exposed, to some unspoken racist attitudes, all of which shocked her greatly. But on the whole, it was a fruitful time for her. She was especially grateful for the fact that a group of people—mostly parents and teachers from the nursery school—founded a support group and took it upon themselves to guarantee Emily a salary for two years so she would have some income during the initial and most difficult years of her children's garden.

The Village of Madietane

Madietane is a small village of a few thousand people, situated in a rural area in northern Transvaal, tucked between mountains that rise like humpbacked giants in an otherwise flat landscape. Madietane is part of the self-governing homeland of Lebowa and far away from the blacktopped main roads. A visit there—a three-

and-a-half-hour drive from Johannesburg—is demanding on one's vehicle, as one drives for about one hour on rather stony dirt roads.

Upon approaching Madietane, one is received into the most beautiful surroundings. Emily's house and the projects she started are right at the foot of the mountains, with huge boulders spread over the mountain sides as well as in the valley below. The foothills are dotted with aloes looking like mini-trees. The area resembles a park landscape, not man-made, but directly offered by nature.

The language spoken in this area is Northern Sotho (pronounced "Sutu"), belonging to the Sotho group of languages, spoken by about one third of the black people in South Africa. The people in Madietane call themselves Pedis.

If one walks across the land given to Emily for the development of her education project and reaches the graveyard, one sees the name Moabelo on many graveyard stones. And whenever one is introduced to someone, one may hear the name Moabelo. Emily, who herself is a Moabelo, is quite aware of the retarding forces that could come from solely being connected to blood lineage. She tells

us that she and her committee work out of a different impulse—her work stands under the guidance of the archangel Michael, the progressive spirit who is guiding mankind in its development at this stage in time.

The village of Madietane has no electricity yet, as only a handful of people would be able to pay for it. Water must be fetched from a common tap or can be bought per liter. And to make things even more difficult, the area is extremely dry, having many years of drought so severe nothing will grow.

But the people are strong compared to urban dwellers who have been weakened by the "good life." As a child, Emily had to walk for hours to buy groceries. When homegrown beans had to be sold to the grocer, a group of children was organized, each carrying a small bag of beans on his or her head. After their long walk, they were rewarded with a slice of bread with some sugar on it. The only time money was spent on bread was at Christmastime or at a similarly special occasion. Though people are strong, they are not as strong any more, says Emily, as when she grew up. By their own admission, her children would not be able to do what she did in her youth.

Obstacles Against a New Educational Impulse

Although Emily is a Northern Sotho, she carries the wisdom of a world citizen. There is absolutely nothing narrow-minded about her. She knows what needs to be done and she goes about doing it. Emily is trying to bring a new educational impulse to a world where most things are still done in traditional ways: One is not to question authority, regardless of whether or not this authority is an older person, the chief, or the government. Such a situation is rife for conflict.

Many young people—calling themselves "the comrades"—at times take things into their own hands. Emily is performing a difficult balancing act to keep good relations with both sides of the power struggle. Mostly, she agrees with the changes the comrades want to see happen, but she also sympathizes with the older generation and their ways.

A problem for Emily was not being allowed to form her own school committee and being dependent on a community that elected specific people for her committee. As can be expected, certain people are helpful and able to further the cause, whereas others do not grasp the implications of such a new educational concept.

Another problem is the adoration people have for certificates and diplomas. The belief is the more diplomas or certificates, the higher the salary. Thus, certification becomes a status symbol. Some in the community are envious of Emily, asking, "why should she think she can do such a thing? She does not even have a degree or a teacher's certificate."

There is one other preschool in Madietane, located in a church just as Emily's is, where the small children are taught by a state certified teacher. It is a regulation in Lebowa that preschools shall be run by qualified teachers, who are paid by the state of Lebowa.

During the first years of Emily's children's garden, Emily was obliged to send her children first to the above-mentioned pre-school before they could be admitted to class I of the local primary school. This pained Emily, as she saw how the children deteriorated in an environment where children are punished for "bad" behavior and given "stones for bread." The emphasis is one-sidedly on intellectual drilling, at a time when the soul life of the young child should be nourished by an imaginative environment.

Emily's philosophy is that the best she can do for her community is to help the children gain confidence in themselves without losing respect for others and, in addition to food for their bodies, give them nourishment for their souls and spirits. Only time will tell how children from such remote rural areas respond to Waldorf school methods. Emily's school will most certainly bring new aspects to light.

A bridge needs to be built between the traditional ways of educating children—geared solely toward mastering the practical and social aspects of life—and the academically oriented Western ways of abstract learning that do not include character building through teaching genuine responsibility and social awareness.

Black people feel such urgency about catching up with the white people's way of educating they mostly do not realize how one-sided that way really is. A real bridge can be built between the two educational systems only by thoroughly engaging the children in art and making learning an experience for their total being, so that their feeling life as well as the will life are engaged with the forces of the head.

Emily wants to bring light. The Sotho word for light is *Lesedi.* That is the word Emily chose for her children's garden: Lesedi

Children's Garden. That light will brightly shine out of the eyes of the children who have the opportunity to go through such a schooling process.

Obstacles of the Material Kind

At Inkanyezi in Alexandra, Emily had been working with large groups of children for several years. Now, in the first week, she had 10 children; then, on each day of the following weeks, more and more children were brought to her, until at last she had 135 children, and all of them in the one-room church. She was very fortunate to find good people who wanted to be trained by her and whom she could send to the Baobab Centre for three-week training periods.

The children had to be fed. There was no way Emily could have the children bring lunch boxes to school, as the disparity in food is so great that it would create unhappiness between them.

This entire situation made it necessary for Emily to try raising substantial funds for her school, for a nursery school building, for a kitchen with equipment, and for salaries, if possible. Emily managed to get a two-room prefabricated building surrounded by a fence on part of the plot the chief had allotted to her. A kitchen

was built especially for her school behind the church and furnished with equipment. She also received wooden tables and chairs. Most of the material donations were given by different embassies.

Emily is still struggling to find funds to run the school. Most parents can pay little and often they cannot manage that.

The children have beautiful surroundings for play—much better than in any township environment—but they need toys and playground equipment to develop additional qualities.

The big obstacle to fund-raising is the fact that Emily's project is in such a remote area. Connections to the "big" world are limited and costly, mainly because of the distance. People inclined to provide funds first want to see the place. Emily has to fetch them by taxi from the nearest town and pay for her visitors' taxi ride herself. Naturally, she dreams of having her own minibus with which to shop and take care of various other errands and needs. She can get foodstuffs donated, but because of the transportation problem, she cannot make use of these offers.

To reach Emily by telephone is another major obstacle. One can contact her only via a friend of the school who lives nearby. When Emily began with Lesedi, she handed in a request for a telephone, but so far without success.

Official Opening of Lesedi Children's Garden

August 16, 1991, was the big day for the official opening of the Lesedi Children's Garden in Madietane. This happening was planned well in advance; invitations went out to many people in and outside of Madietane.

Inkanyezi Children's Garden in Alexandra received an invitation too and decided to hire a bus to take a large contingent of children. And, of course, a lot of food had to be prepared, as this is a necessary part for any festive occasion. The evening before the big day we went to a neighboring village to make sure the person who was chosen to be the main speaker was, indeed, prepared to speak. All was in place, and even the people from the TV station were going to come.

When the next day arrived the cooks got busy very early. All the guests coming from afar had been accommodated for the night in the village and needed breakfast. And then the TV people appeared. Luckily, they came early so the interviewes with Emily and Carol, one of the Baobab trainers, could take place before the official opening commenced. After much delay, it seemed that the great moment had come, because all the "important" people had finally arrived.

All gathered at the church, from where we moved in procession to the site of the new building, outside of which a marquee had been erected to protect guests from the scorching sun. The little children, clad in their colorful aprons, walked in the middle and sang the new songs they had learned about their Lesedi Children's Garden. I said "walked," but in actual fact, all of us used ceremonial steps—rhythmically and slowly—to make our way in a formal procession to our destination, the marquee. The whole ceremony had a touch of ritual: the agenda of speakers, the songs, the music, and the children's ring games, the praise songs introducing each new speaker, as well as the main guest speaker.

The main guest speaker was Poppie Mashamaite—also called the Mother of the North—because she is the official supervisor from the Lebowa government and oversees all nursery schools in the area. She spoke very well at this special occasion. This was remarkable since not until the eve of the opening of Lesedi did she learn more about Waldorf educational concepts. Poppie was quite

113

clearly impressed by what little she had heard and seen, by the interaction of the teachers with the children, as well as by the ring games the children performed, partly in English, partly in Sotho.

One by one, the people were introduced by the master of ceremonies, in a most humorous way: the chieftainess and her son, the new chief, the chairman of the committee, and Mrs. Anna Mohlabi, who had started a home for handicapped children and adults and used this opportunity to make a plea for the handicapped. She said, they should be brought out of the backyards and into the open so they, too, might have a chance to develop themselves.

The teachers and children from the Inkanyezi Waldorf Centre in Alexandra contributed by playing their recorders. The friends from Novalis House played instrumental music with flute, violin, and cello. At that, all children in the background stretched their necks, because this was something totally new for them. The Madietane choir sang beautifully. All was very festive, indeed, yet stretching people's attention to the limits.

Finally, all the guests could follow the chief, who, key in hand, was to open the doors of the new nursery school building. That was the moment when the local dance group in their special Sotho

outfits started to beat their drums and dance. They had waited already very long, thinking they would have a captive audience all afternoon. Yes, Emily gladly allowed them some time, although this tradition was not quite in line with the church's.

During successive visits it became clear to me that the old and the new, or the past and the present, live side by side in such a village. The people, still holding on to their traditions, lived in a particular area of the village, mainly on the outskirts. For some reason, they had been ordered by the chief to abandon their houses and come and live in the village where most of the people lived. On the other hand, the people who belonged to the church and who adhered to the Christian faith, lived mostly right at the foot of the mountains, just like Emily.

Eventually, the two groups were to be integrated—the "heathens" and the Christians. The Christians liked to have quiet church services. Now, each Sunday, they were disturbed by the beating of drums next door. As a result, a revival meeting of a whole week was to take place to find out whether or not more people could be won for the Christian faith. I do not know the outcome, but I heard the revival for four consecutive days. It certainly sounded forceful and must have made some impact on the community. After a while, I learned to see in people's faces whether or not they still adhered to the old ways. Each time I talked to Emily about this, she would confirm my impression.

The communal spirit is alive in the people—it is part of their being—but there are enormous differences to overcome between politicized youths and the traditional ways of the chief, between those with certificates and degrees and those without, and last but not least, between the heathens and the Christians. Like every-where else, people must develop understanding and tolerance for each other's ways. We hope that the Lesedi Children's Garden can be a beacon of light indeed!

The result of the TV coverage of the opening of Lesedi was that scores of people who had seen the video approached Emily. She was also invited to do a radio interview. Suddenly, Lesedi was in the limelight and a reality not only for Madietane, but also a future possibility for other village communities.

Further Developments Toward Waldorf Schools in Lebowa

While the developments in Madietane went on, other things

occurred. One day we received a phone call from Ellis, a black businessman from the Pietersburg area not far from Madietane. He had first phoned the *Sowetan*, Soweto's daily newspaper, because he had read articles offering fresh ideas on education. These had been written by Sam Mabe, one of *Sowetan*'s journalists.

Ellis learned that in 1991, Sam had been assassinated in cold blood by an unknown assailant. With all the forces of intimidation, as described in the chapter on township life, it is very dangerous to stand up as an individual and openly speak one's innermost thoughts, especially when they are innovative and free from political manipulation.

Carol, one of the Baobab trainers, had some contact with Sam, as she also was impressed by his frank articles. In fact, they had a long telephone conversation about Waldorf education. Sam was very interested, because he was involved with a private school in Soweto and had developed similar ideas concerning the direction in which education ought to go. He then visited the Michael Mount Waldorf School in Bryanston near Johannesburg.

At the offices of the *Sowetan*, someone was aware of Sam Mabe's contact with Carol. This person was therefore able to give Ellis Carol's telephone number. (It is quite interesting to see how certain connections come about.) Since that time, Ellis visited our projects in Alexandra and had a chance to gain a comprehensive impression of the possible impact of this kind of education. He was greatly influenced by these visits.

Ellis is a businessman, quite pragmatic and full of initiative. Already, he initiated programs to create work for the unemployed. One initiative is a shoe shine, the other a car-wash project.

Of course, Ellis also wants to see better education for children, beginning with early childhood education. In Waldorf education, Ellis found the model he was looking for. He organized funds from local businesses with which he built a nursery school in Ceres near Pietersburg. His wife committed herself to the task of developing this nursery school, and already 80 children are enrolled.

Ellis plans to build more nursery schools and wants to send people for training to the Baobab Centre. We thought it would be important that he and Emily, who are working and living in each other's vicinity, should meet. Ellis paid a short visit to the Lesedi Children's Garden in Madietane, but because of time pressures could not manage more.

On my trip north, I wanted to visit Ellis and his projects. I also hoped it would be possible to arrange a longer meeting for Emily and him. Out of this plan, a remarkable meeting evolved, not only involving Ellis, Emily, and myself, but also Mabel Chueu, Sophie Mabotha, and Poppie Mashamaite, who had been the key speaker at the opening of Lesedi. The entire group wanted the same things: to uplift the communities, to provide nursery schools for very young children, and to convince people to be trained.

Mabel had visited Emily more often and seen for herself that at Lesedi quality education was given the children. In the entire area in which Mabel had formerly worked as a social worker, people cared for children in their own homes, because parents needed to leave their children with someone while they went to work. All those child-minders needed training, if the children in their care were to be furthered in the right way.

Mabel, an elderly lady who, upon retirement, founded with others the Community Development Foundation, was full of desire to help change the social environment in poverty stricken areas. She felt that she had seen and heard enough of Waldorf education to know that Baobab could provide the kind of training the child-minders needed. As she already had 15 child-minders signed up as members of her organization, many children would ultimately benefit from the long-term program of having one person trained who, in turn, would train the others.

Mabel arranged with Emily that, in the meantime, all the child-minders would take turns observing the activities at the Lesedi Children's Garden. Emily immediately saw this would be the beginning of new insights for many people. She realized it would be yet another task, in addition to developing her own nursery school and training her own teachers, all of whom were new to the vast amount of insight that had to be obtained concerning the development of children.

If she were free to dedicate herself solely to the training aspects of her own and other nursery school teachers, things would be quite different. But Emily still had to worry about the salaries for her teachers and about an income for herself and, also, how to obtain more adequate space to accommodate all the children who wanted to come to her.

Thus, quite unexpectedly, we found ourselves congregating in the lobby of the Holiday Inn: five people, all of whom wanted to achieve the same goal, and who lived in the same area or in the same township, Seshego, but who did not know each other.

Everyone, except possibly Poppie Mashamaite, was convinced that Waldorf education was what each wanted for the projects in their care.

At first Poppie heard about the almost ridiculous situation of Emily's children having to go to the official preschool for a whole year before entering primary school. She immediately offered to sort out this predicament in her capacity as the official inspector of all preschools in the area and to sort it out on a humane social level and to encourage the teacher of the other nursery school to meet with Emily.

We saw the strain and worry concerning this difficult situation literally fall off Emily's shoulders. Many black South Africans suffer severely from high blood pressure and this worry quite likely contributed to pushing Emily's blood pressure to unacceptable levels. But Emily still had another arrow in her bow; she explained her plan of having not only a nursery school, but also starting a Waldorf primary school. This venture would, of course, only work if she could convince the Lebowa government that the planned school would establish high standards and employ qualified teachers.

Ellis and Mabel immediately grasped the importance of Waldorf nursery school children remaining in the stream of Waldorf education on entering primary and eventually secondary level schooling. Thus, Ellis promised to see to it—with the cooperation of the other members of the group and help by Baobab—that a structure would be developed for guarding the life of private schools. Furthermore, information would be published to elicit support for the concept and actual implementation of Waldorf education in Lebowa.

Our experience in South Africa is that many people speak straight from the heart. Western education has done great harm by not recognizing that bridges need to be built between the heart and the head. The overemphasis on intellectual learning, while disregarding the need for a transition from the traditional way of learning, strongly influences the development and, ultimately, the character of a person. Not only have people become rigid in their thinking, but widespread corruption has manifested itself as one of the results of this one-sidedness. Therefore, it is extremely important that those initiatives interested in Waldorf education in Lebowa make a concerted effort so they stand strong and unified.

The event related above was truly wonderful: people who had

not known each other until that meeting forged a link to guard the future of their children. Apart from the organizational aspects, there is the major task for Baobab to supply enough understanding of Waldorf education so that what at first happens in the heart will take hold of the cognitive aspect of people as well. As Rudolf Steiner said: "Pedagogy is love for man resulting from knowledge of man."

Already, Emily foresees the consequences of the Lesedi Children's Garden being officially accepted as a nursery school. She knows that many parents would have loved to send their children to her school but hesitated because they did not want their children to experience the traumatic transition of having to go to class I via another preschool applying totally different methods.

The beginning of 1992 saw Lesedi Children's Garden with an enrollment of 120 children. Of these, 89 were ready to advance to class I in the primary school in the beginning of 1993. Unfortunately, Baobab did not yet have enough trained teachers to immediately send two to Madietane. Thus, the parents of these 89 children had to send their children to a DET school but they intend to pull them out as soon as two teachers could be found for them.

Another big event brought even more attention to Madietane and the Waldorf education impulse that tries to be realized there. In November 1992, Emily was chosen "Woman of the Year" as part of the nation-building drive by the *Sowetan* newspaper. All of a sudden, Emily and her far-away rural village have become known to many people. This can only be of benefit to her project.

Needless to say, we are all very proud of Emily and her positive will to bring light to her people.

Emily sometimes wonders how she will cope with the gigantic task she set for herself. But Emily is a deeply religious person. She knows the true source of the strength that helped her through the previous two years when she was able to overcome yet another major problem, this time concerning her own health. However, that has improved in the meantime. Emily really wishes for a person to stand beside her; someone with understanding and life experience with whom she could discuss all matters concerning the children and the community.

In some respect she has found such a person in Sophie Mabotha, who grew up in Madietane but now lives comfortably in a big house in Seshego, the township adjoining Pietersburg. She is a retired hospital matron, full of energy and plans of how to help improve the lot of her people. Sophie has given Emily the house in Madietane where she grew up and that is no longer used by her family. There, Emily can start self-help groups of parents who want to learn new skills and, it is hoped, find meaningful occupations that guarantee an income from manufactured articles as well as some income for the school. Emily already secured three sewing machines!

Another big dream Emily had for Madietane was to see a clinic established and proper health care rendered to the people of the area. The piece of land given Emily is enormous, big enough for several nursery school classes, a primary school, a high school and even a clinic.

Realizing Another Dream

Since the official opening of Lesedi Children's Garden, some additional developments took place.

Eckehardt, a doctor from Germany with South African medical qualifications and 14 years of living experience in South Africa, offered to set up a clinic in Madietane. He is still gathering the necessary practical skills in a clinic in Soweto, but in two years he will be ready to run a full-time clinic in Madietane. Of course, this will require a building and so will the new primary school.

In the meantime, another miraculous thing happened; Tiny Moabelo, one of the first black architects in South Africa listened to the TV coverage of the opening of Lesedi. How amazed he was to learn about these developments in his home village! (The name "Moabelo" must have been a clue that he might be a relative of Emily Moabelo, and he is.) Thus Emily found a new and greatly skilled supporter in Tiny, who already made the architectural drawings for the entire Lesedi primary school plus teachers' housing as well as the new clinic building. Thus, Emily is coming closer and closer to also fulfilling that dream. We certainly can agree with the black American poet and writer Langston Hughes (1902-1967) who urged us to hold fast to dreams, for if dreams die, life is a broken-winged bird that can't fly. Therefore, we say, hold fast to dreams . . .

CHAPTER XIV

INITIATIVE IN THE HOMELAND OF VENDA

The Homeland of Venda

One can be fascinated by the beautiful countryside of Venda and its people. During other trips to the north, coming from the arid landscapes of northern Transvaal, I was astonished to see the growth of lush plants and fruit trees. Although people do not have much money, they nevertheless manage to grow things and have an abundance of fruit: papayas, mangoes, sun-ripened bananas, litchis, and avocados, among other kinds of fruit.

Turning away from the main route between Louis Trichardt and Thohoyandou, traveling south to Vuwani and north to Mutale, I discovered that there are also less fertile parts and parts with less rainfall. I also got the impression that the people in these areas seem to form close units.

The area around the Soutpansberg mountains, also referred to as "the land of a hundred streams," were originally inhabited by Bushmen. With invasion by the Vhavenda, beginning in the 12th century, the Bushmen moved south, leaving behind their legacy of rock paintings as well as the nature spirits, revered in streams and waterfalls, lakes and forests.

To this day, each place has its specific legend and those are not stories that one can easily forget. The world of imagination is alive and shines from the people's eyes almost magically. Yet, these people appear to have been able to connect the modern ways of life with the old traditions. Life seems well organized and peaceful.

A Home in Venda

In the summer of 1991 I had the opportunity to visit Flora, one of the doll makers at Alexandra, at her home near Vuwani in Venda, where she went for the Christmas holidays.

When Flora initially came to us, together with her husband Elias, whom we had employed as caretaker of the Inkanyezi Waldorf Centre in Alexandra, we knew that both were living with their two children in a corrugated iron hut of only three-by-three meters. We offered them a space of three-by-six meters in the big Zozo hut. At times, they accommodated another couple for many weeks or months on end, because that couple had nowhere else to go. Flora and Elias had hardly any furniture and stored away any odd item they found, because it might come in handy some day. This was the only experience we had of the way in which our caretaker's family lived in Alexandra.

How astonished was I, therefore, to see their home in Venda! They have one big rondavel as a sleeping and living place, complete with twin beds and a beautiful dining set comprising a large wooden table and chairs. There are cupboards with hanging space and shelf space and religious pictures on the walls. The second rondavel is the cooking place—we could call it the kitchen. There was the fire on the floor on which Flora was preparing a meal for her guests. When all was ready, she served tea with bread,

later *mealiepap* (Afrikaans word for boiled mash of maize) with meat, and everything in the most gracious way. While I was admiring the beautiful hand-crafted items in the rondavel, from bedspreads to pillowcases to tablecloths, Flora got up and handed me two beautiful items she had made. It is Venda tradition that a guest never goes home empty handed.

How limited had been my picture when I saw Flora and Elias in their situation in Alexandra! Because there was no job for cash available for them in Venda, they had to look for work elsewhere. But Venda is their real home where they live like a king and queen. Never mind that there was no toilet—nature is all around, so there is no need for such an amenity; never mind that water has to be fetched in wheelbarrows, and candles have to be used for lighting; never mind that one has to be away for most of the year. Here, they own a big plot, build their own houses, pay no taxes and live in peace and agreement with their neighbors.

It was satisfying to see Goodwill, Flora and Elias' daughter, in her own environment at least once. She is in Lorna's class and extremely shy. When Goodwill's elder sister gave me a glass of water, while bending down deeply and remaining on her knees, I understood even more deeply that different customs prevail in different areas. To understand the behavior of a child, one really has to understand his or her whole background and upbringing.

A few months later, I am able to say that my visit to her real home has made a tremendous difference in Goodwill's performance in class. She has become open and communicative and is a bright, hard-working pupil, because a link between home and school had been forged. I am increasingly keen to visit some of the other doll makers at home. I am sure that it will be as revealing as was my visit to Flora and Elias' home in Venda.

How beautiful life in nature's surroundings at Venda can be became obvious on another occasion, namely Caroline's wedding and our visit to her nursery school, Tsingandendede, in Mutale, Venda.

Tsingandendede Nursery School in Mutale, Venda and a Wedding

It does take time, if one is not from Venda, to learn such complicated names. But that is the name Caroline gave to the nursery school she started in Mutale and so we had to familiarize ourselves with it. The word *Tsingandendede* is the name of a circle game in Venda language.

Our plan was to visit the Waldorf nursery school Caroline had begun in Mutale. She had been working at Inkanyezi Children's Garden in Alexandra for about 18 months and after that at the Waldorf Crèche of Pharma Natura (mentioned in chapter 3) in Wynberg near Johannesburg. In addition, Caroline attended several in-depth training courses on early childhood education, offered by the Baobab Centre.

It was clear that she was a person of responsibility and initiative. One day, Caroline announced that she was going back to Venda to start a Waldorf nursery school there. It was a courageous deed, as Venda is far away—a six-hour drive from Johannesburg—and she would not be able to count on any support system, for the time being.

Bit by bit, we received word through her fiancee, Godfrey, who still worked in Johannesburg, that Caroline had been given a private house to use for the nursery school and that she had already 50 children in her care. When we met with her during one of her trips to Johannesburg, it was clear that her task had turned out to be more difficult than she had imagined.

As had been the case in Emily's environment in Lebowa (described in chapter 13), Caroline encountered much ignorance and distrust, but also great interest. She was asked to speak publicly on several occasions, especially in churches, and gradually the conviction grew that possibly there was something worthwhile in the kind of education Caroline attempted to introduce.

We had not yet been able to visit Caroline's place. Finally, when the opportunity arose to travel there in the summer of 1991, we heard that instead of seeing the Tsingandendede Children's Garden, we could be present at her wedding. It seemed a wonderful opportunity to find out more about the customs of the land. Our presence on that very special day in her life would make Caroline feel supported. And so it was possible for Caroline and her family as well as for myself and a pediatrician from Germany, to be present at her wedding. We thoroughly enjoyed ourselves and felt welcome at this big gathering of black people.

The wedding was to take place under a huge tree in the open veld, with a marquee providing shade for the bride and bridegroom, for the retinue of 12 young people (six young women and six young men), and for the special guests. The men were to be seated on one side, the women on the other.

At exactly the appointed time, six decorated cars arrived, driving up with loud hooting. Then the same type of procession took place as the one described in connection with the opening of Emily's school. With the bride and bridegroom—each accompanied by the witnesses positioned in the first two places and the six young couples in their special outfits behind them—the procession moved slowly with rhythmical side steps, accompanied by the local band, in direction of the canopy.

It would be beyond the scope of this book to describe all the rituals, except that bride and bridegroom had to sit apart until the actual wedding ceremony had taken place and up to that moment, the bride had to keep her face and eyes downcast. Because of this, we did not know whether or not Caroline was aware of our presence.

The older women, mostly dressed in the special Venda costume with numerous metal rings around their arms and ankles, danced their dance, all the while cleaning the road of marriage with palm fronds so that all would be smooth for Caroline and her husband.

One can see how customs dictate that each rite of passage in the lives of the people should become a festive ritual for the whole community to witness. For any of those festive happenings, a big meal must be provided for all the guests. Although this may put people in debt for many years to come, things shall be done in the right way.

Before the meal could be served, the whole wedding party was taken to a special place, quite far away. The secret was kept until we arrived in a mountainous area where we found ourselves suddenly transplanted into a fairy-tale landscape. We climbed onto the rocks and saw a most beautiful waterfall splashing from high up into a basin. While photos were taken of the married couple, the wedding party, and the different guests, the little boys went for a swim in the pool farther down below the waterfall. Caroline told us that this had always been her favorite spot and that her fondest childhood memories had to do with this place.

We felt privileged to have been allowed to be a part of all this and to share Caroline's and Godfrey's happiness. In time to come, we knew we would continue to be connected through her initiative, the Tsingandendede Children's Garden.

CHAPTER XV

INITIATIVES IN CAPE PROVINCE
ARISING FROM BAOBAB

Pauline's Move to Cape Town

In 1989, we were faced with the fact that David and his wife Pauline, about whom we have been writing already in relation to Emily (in chapters 5 and 13), planned to move to Cape Town. Having been so involved with our work as a Baobab trainer and carrying the impulse so strongly, Pauline was determined to continue in the townships in the Cape Town area.

Pauline's own impulse was strongly oriented toward hand-work. She always felt that work done with the hands greatly stimulates the entire learning process. In the beginning, Pauline successfully introduced creative handwork with classes of children in one particular school. The children were happy to be allowed to be really creative as well as to make useful items such as handwork bags or pillow cases. After this initial experience, it was essential that larger groups of teachers would understand the importance of handwork for children and develop confidence in their own creativity.

Upon her arrival in Cape Town, Pauline immediately began to be mentor and liaison for the students we had sent for training to Novalis College: Dudu (mentioned in chapter 10) and Lucky (mentioned in chapter 16) in 1989 and Queen (mentioned in chapter 9) and Mosidi (mentioned in chapter 7) the following year.

In 1991, Dudu finished her two-year training at Novalis College. Feeling strongly connected with Baobab yet wanting to stay in Cape Town, she started getting involved with Pauline's work. Dudu wanted to find out where her specific qualities could best be utilized. She knew it would have to be in the social sphere. Before Dudu became involved with Baobab Centre and the training at Novalis College, she had been a community worker, mainly working with adults.

Another person feeling attracted by Pauline's work was Trevor. Besides being a builder and carpenter, he also had two years' experience as a nursery school teacher after completing the foundation year at Novalis College.

Pauline also made contact with other organizations that worked in early childhood education and community development. A group of friends was organizing an arts and crafts program for children in Khayelitsha and help was needed, because more and more children were eager to take part.

The Activity in Gugulethu, Cape Province

In addition to work in Khayelitsha, there were connections to a project in Gugulethu. Nonkululekhu had started a crèche/nursery school, called Noxolo Children's Garden, in her own house with about 25 children. After coming into contact with the Waldorf education concept, she knew with absolute certainty that this was the direction she wanted to take.

The possiblity then arose for her to go to Holland for training. Although she was quite homesick during her stay overseas, she nevertheless took every opportunity to learn as much as possible. Upon her return, she asked the Baobab Centre to help her set up a whole-day workshop for other child-minders and nursery school teachers in Gugulethu. The workshop became a joint venture between Baobab Cape Town and Baobab Johannesburg.

As the theme was "Nature speaks to the child," we asked all participants to introduce themselves by talking about a natural object, such as a feather or a stone, a bushel of grass or some woolen object, any of which they had chosen before entering the room in which the workshop was to be held.

We were thrilled to see how original and philosophical the participants were in their relationship with nature. With several of them, some cherished childhood memories surfaced; others compared the natural objects with people's behavior. It was delightful to experience the precious "gifts" people brought to the workshop.

When human beings are acknowledged, they feel much more comfortable to share what they experienced themselves as children, and what they now experience with the children in their care. People who later in life really care about the environment were taught reverence for nature in their childhood years. One can hardly stress enough the importance of instilling in children a deep love for the earth and for nature.

This and other training courses were conducted in the new Community Centre in Gugulethu. Novalis College had been asked to help the community work out what was really needed in terms of health care and education facilities. In the end, people from the community themselves made the decisions and provided some architectural suggestions that were then carried out by a team of architects.

The outcome was a beautiful, yet functional building with the most unusual organic forms. Even the builders were excited about the opportunity of becoming creative themselves. This was not just another job—this was their building that had to become as useful and beautiful as possible. The idea behind this whole undertaking was the more the community is involved in a project, the more it will protect it.

Baobab Johannesburg had started the Inkanyezi Waldorf Centre in Alexandra as a pilot project; Baobab Cape Town wanted to follow a similar route. As it turned out, working with Nonkululekhu and the Noxolo Children's Garden was the best starting point.

For a long time, Nonkululekhu had contemplated the idea of building an extension to her very small garage, once she returned from Holland after her stay of three months. She did not return only filled with new ideas and fancy toys she had made with her own hands, such as a mother-earth-doll, and moving pictures made from plywood, or having learned to play the lyre, a harplike string instrument. (The lyre was used by the ancient Greeks and redeveloped in 1926 by Lothar Gärtner and Edmund Pracht. It is frequently used in Waldorf schools and in homes for handicapped children.) Nonkululekhu also returned from Holland with a considerable amount of money that people there collected for her so she could start building the extension to her garage.

At her return to Gugulethu, Trevor offered his expertise in building, which resulted in a most unusual design—a nursery school with rounded doors and windows, reminiscent of the rondavel house black people in rural areas are accustomed to.

Although this extension will help create a spacious nursery school, Nonkululekhu's wish is to have a nursery school built on a separate piece of land and to develop it into a Waldorf school. Her own house would then be used for the very young children of the crèche and for training purposes. To have a big, beautiful school building is a dream of the children of the Noxolo Children's Garden. At present, Nonkululekhu is busy securing a site for this dream to be realized.

If one knows the conditions in townships like Gugulethu and considers the potential of such an initiative, one hopes businesses would want to invest money in such projects where children are led to unfold the potential that lies within them. Not only are the inhabitants of such townships extremely poor, they are also deprived of culture. Waldorf education does not merely offer quality education, it stresses the importance of culture and of celebrating festivals. Beyond reaching and teaching its children, a Waldorf school's life and work usually cause a ripple effect on many levels of the community.

Baobab in Cape Town

The Baobab friends in Cape Town are also deeply involved with the Houtbaai squatter camp. Their investment in that community has already made a big difference. How much more could one help, if people would get a really proper training of at least one year! We are excited about the developments in Cape Town and want to support our friends as much as possible. For that reason, Baobab Centre in Johannesburg was prepared to give the "Capetonians" support, with the understanding that their own fundraising efforts would have to bear fruit after some months.

130

CHAPTER XVI

BAOBAB CENTRE BECOMES
BAOBAB COMMUNITY COLLEGE

Growth of Nursery School Initiatives

Since its inception in 1986, Baobab Centre grew steadily. Teacher training courses increased, and course participants became quite actively engaged; they were intent on trying the new ways in their daily practice as child-minders, nursery school, or primary school teachers. They understood that thorough familiarization with this innovative kind of education was necessary before it could be fully realized.

It was during a meeting with members of the different initiatives in April of 1988, that the name *Isigodi Segolide* (Zulu for golden circles, mentioned in chapter 10) was coined. Each initiative considered itself a golden circle, whereas all of them combined formed one large golden circle. As their organizations grew, the members wanted to gain clarity regarding their relationship to the Baobab Centre and to the Centre for the Art of Living.

Baobab was prepared to assist in ways such as the development of community structures of the schools and in-service training. By becoming associate members of the Centre for the Art of Living, the independent initiatives would send representatives to the Consultative Council, could use the fundraising number of the Centre for the Art of Living Educational Trust, and be under the legal umbrella of the Trust.

Until the end of 1990, several initiatives had been taken up by course participants concerning Waldorf nursery schools, with the idea of expanding into primary school education. Besides conducting courses and workshops and trying to stay in touch with educational developments in this country and elsewhere, the Baobab Centre was now involved with a network of nursery schools in the Transvaal, Natal, and Cape Province.

All initiatives had the intention of expanding into Waldorf primary schools and, eventually, into Waldorf high schools. We had to prepare for that well ahead of time, in order to provide these initiatives with their founding teachers.

At the same time, we had been asked by the students of the three-week intensive nursery school courses to make it possible for them to have a full year's training course.

Increase in Student Enrollment

In January 1991, we had seven people who wanted to be trained as Waldorf teachers. As a start, we envisioned a one-year training course, but it soon became clear to the students that they needed two years, at least. From the beginning we were amazed by their creative abilities and their understanding of the essentials of Waldorf education. Most of them had an incomplete education, partly because of the inferior quality of black education and partly because of all the interruptions caused by intimidation and upheavals in the townships. The students responded very well to a training that included much artistic and practical work with children.

The year 1992 already saw an enrollment of 27 students between the preschool, first-year, and second-year primary teacher training. Six of the preschool students already started three nursery schools with two teachers each. At the beginning of 1993, the number of students increased even more. We now have 40 students in training.

It will be an important task to obtain the necessary accreditation for all our training courses. But, first, it is important to establish a good track record.

The Need for Additional Training

It is also very important to link up with other community colleges that have come into being. We are adamant that the word *community* will not be just a word or an empty shell, but that the community will take an active part in the development of the college. The fact that the college is located in Alexandra and not in a white area reflects our seriousness concerning community participation.

Most of the students come from far away. For that reason,

college hours can only be from 9 a.m. to 3 p.m. Providing accommodations for the students would make it possible to extend the training hours, but then living expenses would be very much higher, as the students would not have the benefit of living at home.

All those deliberations seemed simple when we had only seven students. In 1991, it was still possible to find student loans for the seven students. They could not afford any fees themselves. Now, however, we decided that all students should pay at least one third of the tuition and make a serious effort to raise the other two thirds. They already have many ideas about how they will go about generating some income, for example, making eurythmy shoes, selling hand-painted T-shirts with the Baobab tree on it, organizing Saturday morning schools in the Waldorf way, giving dramatic performances, doing lazur wall-painting of houses, or becoming cashiers at the new market in Alexandra.

It seems that the students find it increasingly important to learn concretely about a variety of matters. The aim is for students of the nursery school training program who are leaving the college to be sufficiently equipped to found and run their own nursery schools, to make the wooden and soft toys that are needed, to do fund-raising, to handle finances, to set up a sound bookkeeping system, as well as to work creatively with the children.

The students of the teacher training program will also need to acquire these practical and administrative skills. Waldorf schools are run by the College of Teachers, without principals. Thus, the students must have learned all required skills to be efficient in all areas. It is quite demanding to become and be a Waldorf teacher. A Waldorf teacher with blinkers, not open to the world, will never be a genuine or effective Waldorf teacher.

Already in the first semester, the students have to do student teaching. In this way, they are exposed to different kinds of schools from the very beginning of their training. Waldorf schools in white suburbs, township schools, and schools in rural areas are available for those practicals. Along with gaining concrete experience, the students will learn also about ecology, rural development, agriculture, and community development. The host schools, in turn, will benefit from the encounters with the students and the trainers.

The seven students who completed their studies at the end of 1992 are an example of how this kind of training stimulated them.

In January of 1993, four of the seven started first classes in Natal, Soweto, and Alexandra. One is going to Sweden for further training in crafts, one is going into biodynamic farming and one is finishing a horticultural degree.

Growing into the Baobab Community College

As the year 1991 drew to a close, we realized the time had come to train more people over longer periods. It was at that moment that the idea of the Baobab Community College was conceived. Our vision had always concentrated on a training program including arts and crafts, literacy, life skills, and community development, because we believe that intellectual and practical learning should go hand in hand and complement each other. At that point in 1991 we realized more had to be done.

The Baobab Community College is really an inspiring new development in our overall work. Again, we have been fortunate to be able to attract new trainers, such as Eric, for example. In addition to taking one Waldorf class through eight years, Eric can also teach handicrafts and music. He is busy setting up a woodwork and metalwork program, at first for our students, then for young people from the Alexandra community. Eric and Lucky (mentioned in chapter 15), the latter of whom we were able to send to Novalis College in Cape Town for two years, are now building a forge, in which the students themselves will make the tools that are needed for doing copperwork and woodwork. Also, this activity may turn into an income-generating component, as the students will produce practical items and artwork that can be sold.

Martin (mentioned in chapter 3) and Christiane have also joined us, both with long years of experience in Waldorf schools in Germany, Martin as a high school teacher, Christiane teaching eurythmy.

Other trainers joined us on a part-time basis. We have been very fortunate to have had Kent with us for three months. He was able to leave his commitments in Sweden for that period and brings with him rich experiences as a teacher and teacher trainer. The encounter with Kent was mutually fruitful, and he is considering coming back with his wife and children. His wife is a eurythmist and would be able to also teach at the College.

We seem to have an important connection to Sweden and not only in terms of people coming to us. The Swedish government was impressed by Baobab College's work and gave us substantial funding for 1992 and 1993. A separate grant from Sweden allows for students to go for training there or to other training centers in Europe. The first student to have this unique opportunity is Sandile who during his second year of teacher training went to Sweden and came back with bookbinding skills. He will go back again to Sweden to learn additional craft skills.

We realize ever more that the two-year teacher training program will still not be enough and may have to be extended to a three-year training course. And so the Baobab Community College develops out of the realities of the students' needs and capabilities and out of the request for nursery and primary school teachers, at first for our *Isigodi Segolide* initiatives, then later for other Waldorf nursery and primary schools.

We have to plan ahead. The development of a high school for the Inkanyezi Waldorf Centre is only three years away. All Waldorf schools in this country, the two in Cape Town, one in Durban, one in Pretoria, and one in Johannesburg, struggle to get enough Waldorf-trained high school teachers.

The challenges are truly enormous. Genuine reform is necessary on a grand scale. In Alexandra alone, 20,000 children between the ages of six and 20 go to school, leaving 108,000 children in the same age range without any education at all. The problems are gigantic, but they must be tackled qualitatively as well as quantitatively.

This then, for the time being, is our most important task: to provide quality education by training teachers—and, of course, nursery school teachers—in such a way that they become learners for life; that we inspire them and support them in their quest for self-knowledge, so they are able to challenge the children's innate capacities for independence and self-reliance. For the time being, we are dependent on the business community and private sector, here and abroad, for support. We wish our donors to consider themselves partners in this challenge. There is only one direction—to go forward with bold steps. Investment in the children of the country is the best investment any business could think of.

CHAPTER XVII

UBUNTU

What lies before us
And what lies behind us
Are only tiny matters
To what lies within us.

Ralph Waldo Emerson
Self-Reliance

In the chapter about individuality and community we touched on the duality that lives in each human being. We came to the conclusion that we need a breathing rhythm between these two aspects, as each alone is devoid of meaning. There is, however, another duality living in each of us, related to the above dichotomy, yet asserting itself on another level. It is the juxtaposition of the inner and outer man. I would like to add the dimension of the soul directing itself through the senses to the outer world in relation to directing its intentions inwardly.

For me, one of the most outstanding features of the African people is their musical ability. Hearing them sing together, which occurs at any important event, can make one feel transported into another world. Their singing can be so rich and full, so expressive of the inner life of soul, so full of harmony, that one can be only awed by it. One song has touched me deeper than any other: it is the national hymn *Nkosi sikelel' i Afrika* (God bless Africa)— mostly sung first in Zulu and then in Northern Sotho. There is an old African saying: "The spirit will not descend without singing." Music is the heartblood of the African people; it is the sphere where the soul relates to the spirit within. The African soul, it seems, could not exist without this sense of harmony and inspiration; it must feel that music is nearer to the heart of the world than any other art form.

I was so pleased to find this expressed in a poem by Aimé

Césaire, the black writer from Martinique, who describes how his people are seized by the inner rhythm rather than the outer shell and in awe yield themselves to the essence of things.

Which are the qualities that can recognize the essence of things that can be seized by the rhythm of things? Who are those, in Aimé Césaire's words, who are not intent on conquest but would rather play the play of the world? Is it possible that a great part of humanity has been cut off from this more innocent part of its being? Should we say: Africa we need you, or rephrase it to: Africa, I need to find you in myself?

Just recently, I became aware of the profound meaning of the Zulu word *ubuntu*, when I attended the official opening of the Ubuntu Country Market. (The Ubuntu Country Market is held every Saturday at the Max Stibbe School, a Waldorf school in the rural area called Mooiplaas east of Pretoria.) We were told by the main speaker that a prospective bride or bridegroom is accepted by the family only, if the person has *ubuntu*, translated as "true humanity" or "moral quality."

One could say that many who engage in the most horrifying acts of violence, treachery, and bribery have been cut off from this human quality of *ubuntu*. We could, with Alan Paton say, "Cry, the Beloved Country."[19] But we could also try to fathom this deeply seated moral force in the many human beings we meet daily. We could ask ourselves whether or not one-sided intellectual education has been greatly responsible for eroding the innate human qualities, stunting a person's totality.

All the adults involved in the Baobab Community College or in any of the other Waldorf initiatives would like to train teachers and work with children in such a way that they shall not lose the qualities of trust and goodness. Our children have a spontaneity and friendliness that is heartwarming. There are times, after yet another spell of violence and township upheaval, when the children have seen and heard too much. Then, a shadow falls over their being and they cannot play. But the heart of a child is full of forgiveness, full of trust and hope that the world is good after all.

Our main task as educators is to see to it that the children do not lose this *ubuntu* that is so strongly present in the African child, but, in the course of years, must be connected to the light of consciousness. In other parts of the world, the light of consciousness comes more easily, often with coolness and objectivity, while the warmth of the heart has receded into the depths. In Africa, it often is the other way around. A truly holistic education gives children the chance to develop into adults who can possess the warmth of heart as well as the capacity for enlightened and creative thinking. Such adults can respond unwaveringly and constructively to the demands of the times.

Business people, the world over, know that human resources are the most crucial components in the workplace. We "independent" schools can be free and independent from government interference only if we can engage in an interdependent association with the business world. Effective support is needed for an education that develops and strengthens the whole child—the heart, the hand, and the head—so what lies within can be connected to the past and the future. Waldorf education seeks to redeem one-sidedness, not by rejecting intellectual development, but by activating the inner life and, thus, opening doors.

Africa very strongly relates to the heart and soul qualities in the human being. Africa can help us regain what we have lost. That is why we need Africa. There can be neither peace nor prosperity if the citizens of the world do not open themselves for the healing gift Africa has to offer:

UBUNTU

EPILOGUE

The first documentary about the work of the Centre for the Art of Living was written in 1988 under the title: *Stars and Rainbows over Alexandra*. It ended with the words, spoken by Rudolf Steiner at the foundation meeting of the General Anthroposophical Society in 1923:

> That good may become
> What we from our hearts would found
> What we from our heads would guide
> With clarity of vision.[20]

In the five years since 1988, our wish to heed the call of the times has become increasingly urgent, so we now full-heartedly share the more direct part of this foundation verse:

> O Light Divine,
> O Sun of Christ!
> Warm Thou our hearts,
> Enlighten Thou our heads,
> That good may become
> What we from our hearts would found
> What we from our heads would guide
> With clarity of vision.[21]

To this we would like to add a prayer from Africa.

> *NKOSI SIKELEL' I AFRIKA*

Nkosi sikelel' i Afrika	Lord bless Africa
Maluphakamis' uphondo lwayo	Let her horn be raised
Yizwa imithandazo yethu	Listen to our prayers
Nkosi sikelela—	Lord bless
Thina lusapho lwayo	We, her children
Woza Moya	Come Spirit
Woza Moya Oyingcwele	Come Holy Spirit
Nkosi sikelela	Lord bless
Thina lusapho lwayo	We, her children[22]
(Zulu)	

Morena boloka	God bless
Sechaba sa heso	Our nation
O fedise dintwa le matswenyeno	Do away with wars and trouble
Morena boloka	God bless
Sechaba sa heso	Our nation
O fedise dintwa le matswenyeno	Do away with wars and trouble
O se boloke, o se boloke	Bless it, bless it
O se boloke morena	Bless it, Lord
Sechaba sa heso	Our nation
Sechaba sa heso	Our nation[23]
(Northern Sotho)	

NOTES

1. Truus Geraets, *Stars and Rainbows over Alexandra* (Johannesburg: Centre for the Art of Living, 1988).
2. Rudolf Steiner, Ph.D. (1861-1925). Austrian philosopher and educator. Today, his inspirational ideas are alive worldwide in schools, artistic training, clinics, pharmaceutical factories, farms, homes and villages for the handicapped.
3. Chris Foster, "In the Amphitheater of Africa" in *A Time for Heroes* (100 Mile Road, BC, Canada: Integrity International, 1982).
4. Christopher Fry (1907-). English dramatist. From the play: *A Sleep of Prisoners* (London: Oxford University Press, 1951).
5. ODISA. Organisation Development Institute of Southern Africa. Since 1971, the organization has been working in South Africa on developmental processes in individuals, groups, and organizations. ODISA consultants are all members of the Association for Social Development, an international association of human development consultants.
6. Operation Hunger was founded in 1984 to help alleviate hunger in South Africa by distributing food as well as stimulating self-help projects and teaching people how to grow vegetable gardens under harsh conditions.
7. Eurythmy is a form of movement inaugurated in Germany in 1918. Eurythmy is an art form with curative applications, used extensively in the international Waldorf schools. There are eurythmy schools in many countries; training takes four to five years.
8. In 1953, the Bantu Education Act was passed and the system of apartheid education began. All black schools had to be registered separately under the Department of Education and Training (DET). At the same time, all black schools received their own curriculum, inferior to that of white schools.
9. Ingrid Meyer, "Baobabs, Ancient Monarchs of the Savannah" in *The Baobab: Africa's Upside-Down-Tree*, ed. G. E. Wickens (U.S.A.: Little, Brown and Co. in Association with Sierra Club Books, 1989).
10. Frans Carlgren, *Education Towards Freedom* (Peredur, East Grinstead, England: Lanthorne Press, 1976).
11. Mark Mathabane, *Kaffir Boy: Growing out of Apartheid*. An Autobiography (London: Pan Books, 1987).

12. Martin Luther King, *Strength to Love* No. 5002 (Fount Paperback, 1977).

13. Ibid.

14. Arthur Schlesinger Jr., "The Cult of Ethnicity, Good and Bad" in *Time Magazine*, July 8, 1991.

15. Rollo May, American Psychologist. *The Courage to Create* (London: Collins, 1975).

16. Susan Arstall, M.D., "Living into Africa," in *Newsletter: Anthroposophical Society in America,* Spring 1992, pp. 27-29. Dr. Arstall used to work in the casualty/emergency service of the Alexandra Clinic.

17. José and Miriam Argüelles, *Mandala* (Boulder: Shambhala Publications, 1972). Mandala is a sacred visual art form of the East, with universal application.

18. Ingoapele Madingoane, *From Africa: My Beginning* (Johannesburg: Raven Press, 1979).

19. Alan Paton, *Cry the Beloved Country* (New York: Macmillan Publishing Company, 1987).

20. Rudolf Steiner, "Die Grundsteinlegung" in *Die Weihnachtstagung zur Begruendung der Allgemeinen Anthroposophischen Gesellschaft 1923/24*, Gesamtwerk 260 (Dornach: Rudolf Steiner Verlag, 1985).

21. Ibid.

22. Prayer composed in 1897 by Enoch Sontonga of the Xhosa tribe. Originally, it was the official anthem of the Transkei and sung in other parts of South Africa and Africa. Published first in 1934 by Lovedale Press in No. 17 of the *Lovedale Solfa Leaflets.*

23. Sotho addition to the prayer composed by Enoch Sontonga.

BIBLIOGRAPHY

Argüelles, José and Miriam. *Mandala*. Boulder: Shambhala Publications, 1972.

Arstall, Susan. "Living into Africa" in *Newsletter: Anthroposophical Society in America, Spring 1992*

Carlgren, Frans. *Education Towards Freedom*. Peredur, East Grinstead, England: Lanthorne Press, 1976.

Emerson, Ralph Waldo. *Self-Reliance*. New York: Stewart, Tabori, Chang, 1989.

Foster, Chris. "In the Amphitheater of Africa" in *A Time for Heroes*. 100 Mile Road, BC, Canada: Integrity International, 1982.

Fry, Christopher. *A Sleep of Prisoners*. London: Oxford University Press, 1951.

Geraets, Truus. *Stars and Rainbows over Alexandra*. Johannesburg: Centre for the Art of Living, 1988.

King, Martin Luther. *Strength to Love*. Fount Paperback, 1977.

Madingoane, Ingoapele. *From Africa: My Beginning*. Johannesburg: Raven Press, 1979.

Mathabane, Mark. *Kaffir Boy: Growing out of Apartheit*. An Autobiography. London: Pan Books, 1987.

May, Rollo. *The Courage to Create*. London: Collins, 1975.

Meyer, Ingrid. "Baobabs, Ancient Monarchs of the Savannah" in *The Baobab: Africa's Upside-Down-Tree*, ed. G. E. Wickens. U.S.A.: Little, Brown and Co. in Association with Sierra Club Books, 1989.

Paton, Alan. *Cry the Beloved Country*. New York: Macmillan, 1987.

Schlesinger, Arthur Jr. "The Cult of Ethnicity, Good and Bad" in *Time Magazine*, July 8, 1991.

Steiner, Rudolf. "Die Grundsteinlegung" in *Die Weihnachtstagung zur Begruendung der Allgemeinen Anthroposophischen Gesellschaft 1923/24*. Dornach: Rudolf Steiner Verlag, 1985.

—. *Verses and Meditations*. London: Rudolf Steiner Press, 1972.

Whitman, Walt. *Leaves of Grass*. Boston: Thayer & Eldridge, 1860.

INDEX